Single Mothers in Contemporary Japan

New Studies of Modern Japan

Series Editors: Doug Slaymaker and William M. Tsutsui

New Studies of Modern Japan is a multidisciplinary series that consists primarily of original studies on a broad spectrum of topics dealing with Japan since the mid-nineteenth century. Additionally, the series aims to bring back into print classic works that shed new light on contemporary Japan. The series speaks to cultural studies (literature, translations, film), history, and social sciences audiences. We publish compelling works of scholarship, by both established and rising scholars in the field, on a broad arena of topics, in order to nuance our understandings of Japan and the Japanese.

Titles in the Series

Haiku Poetics in Twentieth-Century Avant-Garde Poetry, by Jeffrey Johnson

Literary Mischief: Sakaguchi Ango, Culture, and the War, edited by James Dorsey and Doug Slaymaker

Japan's Siberian Intervention, 1918–1922: "A Great Disobedience Against the People," edited by Paul E. Dunscomb

Truth from a Lie: Documentary, Detection, and Reflexivity in Abe Kōbō's Realist Project, by Margaret S. Key

Japan's Backroom Politics: Factions in a Multiparty Age, by Watanabe Tsuneo, translated and with commentary by Robert D. Eldridge

Japan's Multilayered Democracy, edited by Sigal Ben-Rafael Galanti, Nissim Otmazgin, and Alon Levkowitz

Resilient Borders and Cultural Diversity: Internationalism, Brand Nationalism, and Multiculturalism in Japan, by Koichi Iwabuchi

Traveling Texts and the Work of Afro-Japanese Cultural Production: Two Haiku and a Microphone, edited by William H. Bridges and Nina Cornyetz

Japan Viewed from Interdisciplinary Perspectives: History and Prospects, edited by Yoneyuki Sugita

Single Mothers in Contemporary Japan: Motherhood, Class, and Reproductive Practice, by Aya Ezawa

Single Mothers in Contemporary Japan

Motherhood, Class, and Reproductive Practice

Aya Ezawa

LEXINGTON BOOKS
Lanham • Boulder • New York • London

Published by Lexington Books
An imprint of The Rowman & Littlefield Publishing Group, Inc.
4501 Forbes Boulevard, Suite 200, Lanham, Maryland 20706
www.rowman.com

Unit A, Whitacre Mews, 26-34 Stannary Street, London SE11 4AB

Copyright © 2016 by Lexington Books

Studies of the Weatherhead East Asian Institute, Columbia University
The Studies of the Weatherhead East Asian Institute of Columbia University were inaugurated in 1962 to bring to a wider public the results of significant new research on modern and contemporary East Asia. http://www.columbia.edu/cu/weai/weatherhead-studies.html

All rights reserved. No part of this book may be reproduced in any form or by any electronic or mechanical means, including information storage and retrieval systems, without written permission from the publisher, except by a reviewer who may quote passages in a review.

British Library Cataloguing in Publication Information Available

The hardback edition of this book was previously catalogued by the Library of Congress as follows:
Library of Congress Cataloging-in-Publication Data

Names: Ezawa, Aya, author.
Title: Single mothers in contemporary Japan : motherhood, class, and reproductive practice / Aya Ezawa.
Description: Lanham : Lexington Books, 2016. | Series: New studies of modern Japan | Includes bibliographical references and index.
Identifiers: LCCN 2016010741| ISBN 9781498529969 (cloth) | ISBN 9781498529983 (pbk) | ISBN 9781498529976 (electronic)
Subjects: LCSH: Single mothers——Japan. | Single mothers—Japan—Economic conditions. | Motherhood—Social aspects.
Classification: LCC HQ759.915 .E93 2016 | DDC 306.874/320952--dc23 LC record available at http://lccn.loc.gov/2016010741

In Memory of Barbara Ezawa

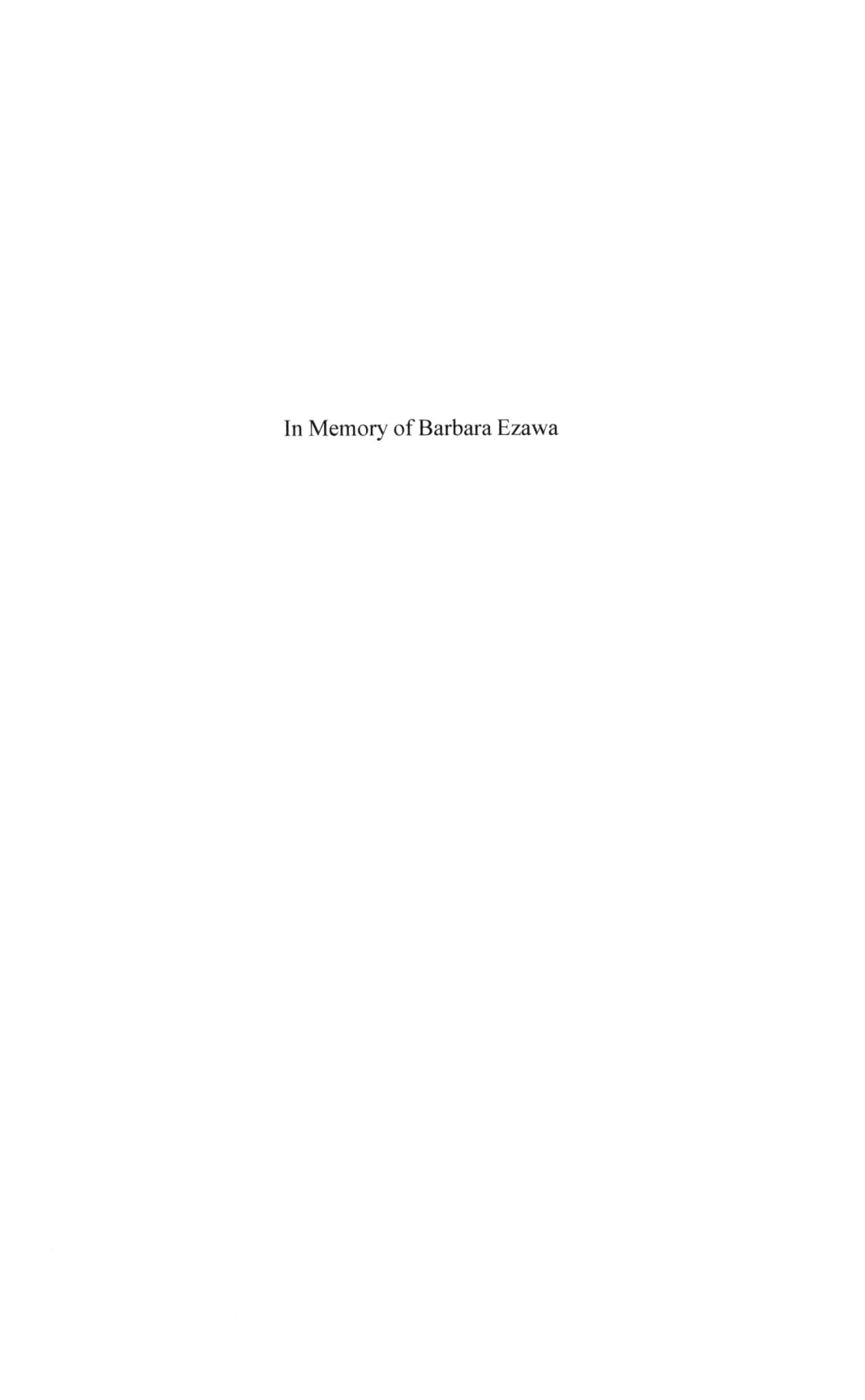

Contents

Acknowledgments		ix
Introduction		xi
1	Single Mothers and the Postwar Japanese Family	1
2	Educational Pioneers	17
3	The Bubble Generation	35
4	Becoming a Single Mother	61
5	Motherhood and Class	83
Conclusion		107
References		117
Index		125
About the Author		129

Acknowledgments

This book has been a long time in the making, and has benefited from the help and encouragement of many. My years as an undergraduate at Sophia University were an important period of exploration and discovery; I am particularly grateful to David Wank for his encouragement to pursue graduate studies, without which I may have never considered an academic career. John Lie, under whose guidance I wrote my dissertation, was unique in combining a deep knowledge of social theory with expertise on Japan, allowing me to freely pursue my research beyond the confines of areas and disciplines. Nancy Abelmann's energetic and enthusiastic presence was an indispensable source of inspiration in bringing this project together. Hiroshi Ishida's guidance, support, and encouragement over many years allowed me to explore the class dimensions of my research on single mothers. I am also grateful for the incisive comments on my research by participants of several research meetings on social class in Japan, organized by Hiroshi Ishida and David Slater.

During my stay in Japan, a series of research meetings with Fujiwara Chisa, Ito Peng, Shimoebisu Miyuki, Shoji Yoko, and Yuzawa Naomi allowed me to gain a deeper understanding of social policy and single motherhood in Japan. The resulting discussions and collaborative projects have been a crucial resource for developing and testing my ideas and insights. Chieko Akaishi's advice and support was instrumental in introducing me to the field, and conducting the research upon which this book is based. Most of all, I am indebted to the single mothers who granted me time for an interview despite their often very hectic schedules. In becoming a working parent myself, I have been fortunate to be able to apply many lessons and insights gained from our encounters.

In the final stages of this project, Carol Gluck and Ross Yelsey of the Weatherhead East Asian Institute at Columbia University offered crucial advice and support in chaperoning me through the publishing process. I am particularly grateful for the comments offered by three anonymous reviewers on earlier versions of the manuscript, and to Melissa Ptacek for her help in polishing the manuscript.

My research in Japan was supported by grants from the Itoh Scholarship Foundation, the Matsushita International Foundation, and a University of Illinois Dissertation Travel Grant. Follow-up research was enabled by an Abe Fellowship, administered by the Social Science Research Council with support and funding from the Japan Foundation Center for Global Partnership. A Netherlands Organization for Scientific Research (NWO) Replacement Subsidy offered precious time to work toward the completion of the manuscript. Parts of chapter 5 were previously published in my chapter entitled "Motherhood and Class: Gender, Class, and Reproductive Practices among Japanese Single Mothers," in *Social Class in Contemporary Japan: Structures, Sorting and Strategies*, edited by Hiroshi Ishida and David H. Slater (Routledge, 2010), 207–17, and are reproduced with permission from Taylor & Francis.

Amidst the challenges of balancing work and family and completing this manuscript, Maxim and Hannah were a source of sustenance, offering theoretical as well as empirical insight into my subject of inquiry. While parenthood rarely mixes well with "productivity," it would have been difficult to write a book on this subject without this experience.

Introduction

Until the onset of the Heisei recession in the 1990s, poverty and social inequality had received relatively limited attention in the study of Japanese family life. As a consequence of the high-speed growth of the early post-World War II economy and the rise of the modern and affluent lifestyle of the salaryman (a white collar employee with permanent employment in the private sector), and his family, postwar Japanese society has been widely considered to be predominantly middle-class (Ishida and Slater 2010). Since the bursting of the economic Bubble and the onset of the long recession, however, inequality in Japanese society and poverty among Japanese families have become important social issues (Abe 2008; 2014; Aoki 2003; Sato 2000; Shirahase 2005; Tachibanaki 2005). As sociologist Masahiro Yamada has argued (2004), with the faltering of the main elements that provided stability to family life during the period of high-speed growth—marriage and the salaryman husband's income—family life has become more unstable and uncertain and families have been bifurcated into "winners" and "losers," dividing those who have achieved the "Japanese dream" of stable employment and a middle-class life from those, including unmarried singles and divorcees, who have not.

Child poverty, moreover, was recognized by the Ministry of Health, Labor, and Welfare as an urgent social issue, as Japan has come to stand out for its high child poverty rate among Organisation for Economic Co-operation and Development (OECD) countries, a result driven largely by the high poverty rate of single mothers (OECD 2006; 2013). In contrast to the image of the happy, carefree, and presumably universal middle-class family life of the heyday of the Bubble economy, recent studies have documented growing disparities in family lifestyle and children's educational opportunities and long-term futures (Hasegawa 2014; Kodomo no hinkon hakusho henshû inkai 2009; Tsuru 2012). In the post-3/11 era, family life is no longer understood simply in terms of the middle class, but now also in terms of the existence of impoverished families and communities that have become even more visible in the course of the events following the earthquake and tsunami that devastated large parts of northeastern Japan on March 11, 2011 ("Nakuso! Kodomo no hinkon" zenkoku network 2012).

In this book, I examine inequality and stratification in Japanese family life based on the life stories of single mothers who raised children during the Heisei recession, which lasted from the 1990s to the early 2000s. Families headed by single mothers constitute only a small minority of families in Japan, yet the experiences of these women offer important insights into persistent inequalities in Japanese family life and into the disadvantages single mothers in particular face in supporting themselves and their children in contemporary Japan. Despite their high work-participation rate, single mothers in Japan have a strikingly high poverty rate, which is not only considerably higher than that of other types of families in Japan but also higher than that of the rate for single mothers elsewhere (58.9% in 2009; Abe 2014, 10). Single mothers' stories allow us not only to recognize the harsh living conditions these people face as individuals, but also to gain greater insight into the structural disadvantages they face as women, workers, and single mothers.

Faced with downward mobility and challenging living conditions as working mothers and heads of household, single mothers' experiences, I argue, offer important insights into the gendered meanings of social class and social mobility. Where education, occupation, and income have been used as standard indicators of social status in social mobility research, the life trajectories of single mothers reveal marital status and maternal practices as central factors that define a woman's social status and class identity. As has been underlined by a number of studies, stay-at-home motherhood has long been promoted by Japanese government policies (Osawa 2002) and continues to be widely considered a social aspiration and a sign of social status, matching that of the middle-class salaryman (Goldstein-Gideoni 2012; Hendry 1993; Imamura 1987). Most single mothers, in contrast, are working mothers, a trend that has likewise been reinforced by government policies (Ezawa 2006; Fujiwara 2005a; Peng 1997). Becoming a single mother in Japan does not only mean having to make ends meet on an often very low salary, but also affects a mother's ability to maintain the everyday practices and family lifestyle associated with the normative ideal of the middle-class mother. Single mothers' difficulties in balancing work and family are not just a practical or a financial matter, but also a question of negotiating the material and social aspects of their gender and class identities.

While aggregate indicators such as education, occupation, and income can map general trends, life-history interviews of single mothers can offer a close-up view of the particular meanings associated with social class and social achievement from a gender perspective. In examining the life trajectories of these women within the broader socioeconomic context of their upbringings and life experiences, we can identify the specific dispositions and orientations that have shaped their life courses and marked their understanding of social status and social achievement. A focus on the life stories of single mothers, therefore, allows us not only to map the individual experiences behind aggregate statistics, but also offers insight into the gendered meanings of social class that inform single mothers' living conditions and strategies for their children's future.

SINGLE MOTHERS IN CONTEMPORARY JAPAN

The term "single mother" in the English-speaking world often evokes the image of an unmarried teenage mother who is the target of fierce criticism of her reproductive practices and her reliance or "dependence" on public assistance or "welfare" (Edin and Kefalas 2005; Fraser and Gordon 1994; Luker 1996). In Japan, by contrast, neither unmarried motherhood nor welfare reliance has been central to public discourse surrounding single mothers. Consider, for instance, the following statement by a single mother and veteran activist, who published her reflections on her experience as a single mother in a journal dedicated to the topic of single mothers' welfare in Japan. She states:

> I [am a single mother and I] live with two children: a freshman in senior high and a sophomore in junior high. The mothers of my sons' classmates always look at their things and say: "You bought a new bicycle—was it a present of some kind?" If I were to say, "Yes, we got it from Grandmother to celebrate his entry into high school," it would not really be an issue, but if I say, "Yes, I just felt like it and bought it," they try to be compassionate and say: "It must have been expensive! You must be in the red this month. Are you alright? What will you do if you get sick? I have a husband who will do whatever is necessary, and I also will have a pension in old age..." (Nonaka 1987, 4).

According to Nonaka, within her social circle, being a single mother appeared to be strongly associated with financial difficulties and downward mobility. Although Nonaka worked full-time, and was able to support herself and her children based on her own wages, she felt scrutinized by married middle-class mothers of her children's school about her ability to afford specific consumer goods. A bicycle not only constitutes a prized possession for a teenager, but also appears as a status symbol, not unlike specific consumer items that have marked middle-class life, such as an air conditioner, car, or color television in the early postwar period (Partner 1999). Nonaka felt pitied by married mothers for her presumed inability to afford the comforts and lifestyle of a middle-class life and for the lack of a breadwinner who would assure her, and her children, of a secure future. Being a single mother in Japan in this case was not just associated with a struggle to make ends meet, but was also considered a departure from the stability and affluence of the normative ideal of the married middle-class housewife. A central characteristic of single motherhood in Japan, therefore, is that it has been associated not only with difficult everyday living conditions, but also with downward mobility and divergence from the postwar Japanese middle-class family ideal.

In other respects, as well, single motherhood in Japan is distinctive. Particularly when compared to other advanced industrialized nations, households led by single mothers remain only a small minority among families in Japan. Whereas single-parent households represent between 10% and 25% of families in most OECD countries (OECD 2011, 28), only 7.4% of households in Japan in 2010 were headed by a single mother (MIC 2010). In addition, whereas a growing number of never-married single mothers has been a key focus of much public debate elsewhere, the same is not the case in Japan. Although Japan's divorce rate has increased steadily in the postwar period, it was initially unusually low, with 0.73 divorces per 1,000 population in 1963. Since the 1990s, however, Japan's divorce rate, with 2.3 divorces per 1,000 population in 2003, has reached a peak and has become comparable to divorce rates in many countries in Europe (MHLW 2004). Approximately 30% of marriages today are expected to end in divorce (Raymo, Iwasawa, and Bumpass 2004). Births outside of marriage, by contrast, even now remain uncommon. Whereas children born outside of marriage constituted between 10% and more than 50% of births in OECD countries in 2011 (keeping in mind that these figures also include children brought up by two unmarried parents; OECD 2011, 25), in Japan this ratio has remained between 1% and 2% of newborns since 1955 (MHLW 2013b). The very marginal presence of children born outside of marriage in Japan today underscores the continuing stigma, as well as the wide-ranging social and economic repercussions, particularly associated with becoming an unmarried mother in Japan (Hertog 2009; Hertog and Iwasawa 2011). As a consequence, most single mothers in Japan are divorcees (80.8% in 2010), and although the share of unmarried mothers (7.8%) among single mothers has been increasing and has surpassed that of widowed mothers (7.5%), it remains comparatively low (MHLW 2011).

That single motherhood is associated with downward mobility and poverty, but not with "welfare dependency," in turn, can in part be attributed to the legacy of single mother policies, which were established in the early postwar period. Single mothers' welfare was a major policy issue in the immediate aftermath of World War II, as the large number of casualties of the war had left many families without husbands, fathers, and sons. In 1947, there were an estimated 1.9 million widows in Japan (Murakami 1987, 228), most of them widowed mothers who had been recently married and who were taking care of small children. The war, moreover, not only contributed to an increase in widowed mothers. The end of hostilities was also marked by an increase in divorces and unmarried motherhood (MHW 1956, 15), the latter of which may be attributed to intimate encounters between Japanese women and members of the American Occupation.

Needless to say, the situation of single mothers in the immediate postwar period was dire. Their educational attainment was minimal (78.1% had completed only elementary school, MHW 1952, 12), and finding stable employment with a feasible income as a mother of small children in the war-torn early postwar economy was challenging, to say the least. Although almost 90% of single mothers surveyed in 1952 were working, their incomes remained extremely low (ibid.). Prewar policies, from the Motherhood Protection Law of 1937 to the pensions for bereaved families of military personnel, were abolished under the Allied Occupation to ensure equality, democratization, and demilitarization. As a consequence, single mothers relied initially on the Daily Life Security Law of 1946, a general public assistance program established to provide support to all persons in need, regardless of social standing (Murakami 1987). Almost half of single mothers qualified for the Daily Life Security Law, but as the allowance in itself was very low and only a little more than a quarter of widows actually received the allowance, mothers remained in very difficult financial circumstances (Aoki 2010; Inoue 1956; Fujiwara 2005a, 116).

However, widowed mothers' pensions and reliance on public assistance did not become the main sources of single mothers' livelihood. Besides the fact that the Japanese state had limited resources to provide livelihood support for all citizens in need in the immediate postwar period, some groups of single mothers also resisted the idea of relying on livelihood support, in particular in the form of public assistance. The nationwide widows movement, the so-called National Widows' Group Association (*zenkoku mibôjin dantai kyôgikai*), played a central role in putting the situation of single mothers on the policy agenda (Aoki 2010; Yamataka 1977). The movement, which included military widows of high social standing, considered the fact that most single mothers had to rely on public assistance for the poor to be humiliating and strongly resisted the idea of remarriage as a solution to their situation (Kawaguchi 2003). Their quest for support was driven by the urge to become independent both from state assistance and from their in-laws, as well as by the goal of escaping the indignity of having to rely on public assistance. In other words, their campaigns for state assistance were motivated not only by the aim of ensuring greater economic independence for widowed mothers, but also by the desire to maintain a certain class status as a single mother. As a consequence, the movement did not call for pensions to "protect" mothers, but rather for a little "help" to allow mothers to make ends meet on their own through work, under the motto "happiness by our own hands" (*waga shiawase wa waga te de*; Yamataka 1982).

The most fundamental characteristic of single-mother policies in Japan, accordingly, has never been the "protection" of maternal care for children, but rather the facilitation of their ability to engage in paid work and to make ends meet on their own. The earliest policies, which continue to be in place to the present day, attempted to reduce their expenses by substantially expanding subsidized housing for single mothers in the form of mother-and-child homes (*boshiryô*) between 1947 and 1958 (Hayashi 1992; MHW 1959) and a low-interest loan program established in 1953 (*boshi fukushi shikin kashitsuke seido*), designed to support single mothers' ability to establish or refurbish their own businesses, acquire professional training, or support their children's education. Single mothers have also been provided with special work opportunities through special privileges for establishing kiosks in public buildings or for obtaining a tobacco and salt selling license (Yamataka 1977).

The last and most significant elements of single-mother policies were added in the late 1950s and early 1960s in the form of the widowed mothers' pension (*boshi nenkin* and *boshi fukushi nenkin*) and the dependent children's allowance (*jidô fuyô teate*) for divorced, unmarried, and otherwise separated single mothers, at a time when political and economic conditions allowed for the establishment of cash assistance programs other than the Daily Life Security Law (MHW 1987; Yamataka 1977). But these measures also aimed to "contribute" to the welfare of children of single mothers, rather than to replace the need for work. Both were too low in amount to cover all expenses, yet helped to top up single mothers' low wages, meaning that most single mothers worked in addition to receiving the allowance. As the dependent children's allowance is a social allowance they are entitled to receive based on their marital status, this has also meant that many single mothers preferred relying on the dependent children's allowance and income from work rather than receiving public assistance, which is associated with considerable social stigma. As a consequence, the work-participation rate of single mothers has remained well above 80% for the entire postwar period, making Japan's single-mother policies among the earliest "welfare to work" regimes (Ezawa and Fujiwara 2005; Fujiwara 2005a; see also Miura 2012).

The legacy of these particular characteristics of single-parent policies in Japan is clearly visible in the work patterns of single mothers in the postwar period. Single mothers in Japan have a very high work-participation rate not only compared to single mothers elsewhere, but also compared to married mothers in Japan, despite the fact that work-participation rates of single mothers tend to be lower than those of married mothers in most other countries (Kilkey and Bradshaw 1999; Uzuhashi 1997a; 1997b). As many as

70.0% of single mothers of a one-year-old child and 88.5% of single mothers of a five-year-old child are working, whereas only 38.2% of married mothers of a one-year-old and 68.7% of married mothers of a five-year-old do so (JIL 2013, 18). This high work-participation rate can in part be attributed to the rather limited reliance on public assistance among single mothers in Japan (16.2% in 2011; MHLW 2012a). Instead, most single mothers in Japan rely on the dependent children's allowance: of the estimated 1.2 million single mothers in Japan in 2010 (MHLW 2011), 755,972 (approximately 60% of single mothers) received the dependent children's allowance (MIC 2015). As the allowance is not aimed at covering all living expenses and has been subject to a number of cuts in recent years (Ezawa and Fujiwara 2005; Fujiwara 1997), income from work constitutes the majority share—specifically, 73.5% of single mothers' overall household income (MHLW 2013a).

The main issue facing single mothers in Japan, therefore, is not access to employment or welfare reliance, but the fact that full-time employment does not guarantee a living wage. Income inequality between two-parent and single-parent families has been increasing due to the growing presence of dual-income families: while the average income of households with children was ¥6.73 million (US$61,182) per year in 2012, single-mother families earn on average less than half this amount (¥2.43 million/US$22,090) (MHLW 2013a). Single mothers who do not reside with their extended family have been estimated to have a 65% to 70% chance of living in poverty (Abe 2005). Since remarriage rates in Japan remain particularly low for divorced women (with only 7.72 remarriages per 1,000 divorced women per year; IPSS 2012), being a single mother in Japan is, therefore, in most cases not a temporary condition, but rather is a long-term situation that has considerable implications for mothers' and children's well-being and socioeconomic status.

MOTHERHOOD AND CLASS

What exactly constitutes women's social class status, however, is a complex question. Since women, particularly in earlier studies of social mobility, have not been included in the Japanese national survey on social mobility (Ishida 1993), and a married woman's class status is interdependent with that of her husband, a woman's education, occupation, and income do not provide clear indicators of her class status. From Pierre Bourdieu (1984; 1987), however, we know that class is not just a matter of economic capital, but also includes a wider constellation of social, cultural, and symbolic elements. Class, according to this view, consists not only of differences in material wealth but also generates a situation with similar conditions, which lead to similar dispositions and cultural practices. Class positions and boundaries are not only derived from material conditions and relations of production, but also are created through struggles to define class identity and its representation in everyday practice. Class is thus not merely an objective position, but consists of subjective perceptions and representations of identity and difference. Lifestyle choices—such as the role of the "professional" housewife—in this sense serve as symbolic representations of class as well as sites where class positions and distinctions are contested and transformed.

To be sure, there has also been considerable discussion surrounding the question of the relationship between gender and class in Bourdieu's approach (McCall 1992; McLeod 2005; McNay 1999; Skeggs 1997). Feminist scholars, among others, have critiqued the androcentric dimensions of Bourdieu's approach to social structural positions, as it defines position based on occupation and does not fully explore the gendered dispositions that define the meanings of different forms of capital (McCall 1992). Recent scholarship has, therefore, explored the possible role of different forms of capital as they pertain particularly to gender—such as emotional capital, embodied capital, and female and feminine forms of capital (Fujimoto 2004; Huppatz 2009; McCall 1992; Reay 2004). An exploration of women's capital investment strategies, likewise, has been suggested as a means of grasping women's subjectivity and agency (Lovell 2000).

In addition, Bourdieu's approach has been critiqued for treating gender as subordinate to class, even if it recognizes differences in gender roles and division of labor depending on class location. While women's positioning is touched upon, they appear as capital-bearing objects rather than capital-accumulating subjects (Lovell 2000). The family, likewise, is recognized for its role in the maintenance of the social order through social and biological reproduction, but Bourdieu's concept of family remains rather static and relies on a narrow and homogeneous model of family (Silva 2005), leaving aside non-traditional family forms and the changing dynamics of family life. In short, while Bourdieu has engaged with the topic of gender and family (Bourdieu 1984; 2001), the relationship between gender and different forms of capital as well as the class dynamics of family life remain insufficiently explored.

There are, however, also empirical applications of Bourdieu's approach that showcase the possibilities of exploring the gender dimensions of class and women's mobilization and negotiation of different forms of capital. Lawler's (1999) analysis of upwardly mobile working-class women, in particular, demonstrates how class can be configured through cultural and symbolic capital as well as artifacts, going beyond economic capital as the most definitive determinant of class status. For instance, working-class women who have achieved a middle-class status by virtue of their employment, income, or marriage, feel acutely the centrality of class-based knowledge and competence in making "right" and "tasteful" judgments when it comes to such issues as parenting and lifestyle choices: food, clothing, and extracurricular activities. Should the child eat simple but hearty meals of red meat and potatoes, as recommended by grandmother, or instead eat whole-grain bread and pasta with plenty of fruit and vegetables, including some superfoods? Such lifestyle choices, particularly when it comes to parenting and food, not only differ by class and generation but also are accompanied by a symbolic social hierarchy that marks non-middle-class lifestyles as "Other." Working-class mothers, then, not only engage in parenting with different resources—cultural and economic—but also need to negotiate their deviation from the middle-class norm, as their parenting practices as well as their own lifestyles and practices lack the same kind of legitimacy as those of middle-class mothers.

Viewed from this perspective, middle-class motherhood, symbolized in Japan by the role and lifestyle of the full-time housewife (Goldstein-Gideoni 2012; Hendry 1993; Imamura 1987), constitutes not only a social ideal or a lifestyle facilitated by the income and status of her salaryman husband. Middle-class mothers' reproductive practices, it can be argued, highlight class-specific dispositions and strategies in the form of specific knowledge and parenting practices, which are not only an expression of specific cultural values but are also deployed and contested as a means to assert and maintain a middle-class status for their children. Reproductive practices, in this context, do not merely constitute ways of ensuring a healthy upbringing for children, but can be read as expressions of class, and cultural capital, as well as a means for the reproduction of class.

Single mothers, from this perspective, offer a fruitful space through which not only to shed light on inequalities and stratification in family life, but also to come to a closer understanding of the gender dynamics of social class in contemporary Japan. Women who become single mothers experience major shifts in their material and social conditions, from changes in their financial resources to new constraints on their lifestyle and mothering practices. Their practices and interpretations in coming to terms with their situation allow us to explore both their dispositions toward and understandings of motherhood and class and their strategies of asserting or maintaining their gender and class identities. That is, precisely because single mothers are not living in a typical two-parent, middle-class family arrangement and face downward socioeconomic mobility, they offer a unique window on the family as a social space where cultural capital is reconfigured and social identities and life trajectories are formed.

ON METHOD

At the heart of this book are fifty-nine life-history interviews I conducted with single mothers in Tokyo between September 1998 and July 2000. Most of the mothers had recently separated and were taking care of preschool-aged children. To get a fuller sense of single mothers' experiences, I also conducted fieldwork, participating in meetings and events of single-mother organizations and visiting public institutions that provide services to single mothers. Recruited by means of a snowball sample, my interviewees cannot represent a larger population of single mothers; yet they do capture the experiences of mothers from a range of backgrounds. Furthermore, in the summer of 2004 and fall of 2005, I returned to Japan for follow-up research, reinterviewing some of the women I had met between 1998 and 2000 and also extending my research to single mothers with older children. These life stories, therefore, offer insight into divorced and unmarried single mothers' living conditions during the Heisei recession, an important historical period characterized by a rise in unemployment and unstable employment and by significant cuts in social assistance to single mothers.

Besides offering insight into single mothers' living conditions during a period of significant social and economic change, the life-story approach also allows us to bring into view the structural location of single mothers in Japanese society. One of the challenges of conducting a study of single mothers is that unlike other disadvantaged groups, such as foreign workers, day laborers, the homeless, or racial and ethnic minorities, single mothers can be difficult to locate in a particular site, such as a segregated residential district or community or a specific school or workplace, where one might conventionally locate an ethnographic project. With the exception of public dormitories provided for mothers with children (*boshi seikatsu shien shisetsu*), single mothers in Japan live mostly in geographically dispersed and often socially isolated conditions. The life world they share with other single mothers consists, therefore, of a social-structural location, rather than a shared physical one. Life-history interviews provide a unique means not only to document individual experiences, but also to examine the structural underpinnings and mechanisms that shape life trajectories (Bertaux and Bertaux-Wiame 1981; Bertaux and Kohli 1984; Bertaux and Thompson 1997). A comparison of life stories, which occur seemingly in isolation, can reveal patterns of experiences that are specific to single mothers and thereby describe the shared social space they occupy in contemporary Japanese society.

A qualitative approach to social class and mobility not only captures a snapshot of current conditions, but also allows us to map the social origins and family upbringing of an individual, which thereby provides a close-up view of the specific family dynamics and societal experiences that have shaped that person's life trajectory. A consideration of the experienced character of family life is especially crucial for an understanding of women's life trajectories. While we understand that class, in the form of a father's occupation, is taken as a leading indicator for a child's future class status, gender complicates this, in that in Japan daughters are less likely to step into the footsteps of their fathers, and educational attainment and employment of daughters differ from those of sons (Brinton 1993; Ishida 1993). A qualitative inquiry into family life promises to offer insight into the "black box" of the family, as well as into the more specific conditions, orientations, and experiences that shape gendered life courses (Bertaux and Thompson 1997). Such inquiry promises to offer insight into the factors which allow some women to pursue opportunities that others do not. Viewed from a gender perspective, class differences are defined not only by the occupation and income of a father, but also by the everyday and family experiences that shaped a woman's habitus and her specific dispositions toward education, employment, and marriage.

A life-history approach also allows us to take into consideration the role of individual agency, as well as of resources, strategies, and perceptions, and the potential impact of these on a person's life course. A specific social position is not necessarily predetermined by material conditions, but is also associated with class-specific dispositions as well as with mobilization of various forms of capital. Such a focus allows us to move beyond a more deterministic perspective on social mobility and instead to explore the potential role of specific strategies and dispositions in shaping women's life courses. My objective is thus not merely to map the experiences and structural location of single mothers, but also to explore the gender dynamics and class-specific strategies that inform their everyday life and life trajectories as single mothers.

THE SAMPLE

The most basic denominator of the group of women who are the focus of this study is that they are mothers who separated from their partners and faced the challenge of raising one or more children in the absence of the biological father. Of the fifty-nine mothers I interviewed, the majority (thirty-eight) was divorced, while eleven were unmarried, and four were widowed; six mothers were separated due to other reasons. But while most analyses of single mothers (e.g., Hertog 2009) focus either on divorcees or on never-married mothers, classification by marital status is not as clear-cut as it may appear. As the existence of the category of "other" that is used in the national survey on single-parent families (MHLW 2011) indicates, the actual circumstances of separation are often more complex. Also, empirically the distinction between divorced and unmarried mothers is often difficult to make. For instance, some mothers lived in common-law marriages, considering themselves married but with no papers documenting their marriage or divorce. While such mothers share some experiences with divorcees when ending their long-term relationship, they lack the legal documents to claim benefits that, during the period of this research, only applied to divorcees, not to "unmarried mothers." A number of divorcees, in turn, rushed into marriage when finding themselves pregnant, in order to ensure their child's legitimate status, but divorced shortly after giving birth and never actually experienced marital life. Some unmarried mothers also expected to marry their partners when they became pregnant, but were unable to do so. Yet another group of mothers, moreover, did get married, but gave birth outside of marriage after the end of a childless marriage. Mothers who gave birth outside of marriage, therefore, are not necessarily "never-married" but rather "unmarried" mothers. The legal marital status of a single mother is therefore a quite arbitrary way of differentiating and classifying single mothers and a poor indicator of the attitudes, lifestyles, and living conditions of these mothers and their children.

Mostly in their thirties and forties at the time of the interview, most of the women were employed and most of these were working full-time. More specifically, of fifty-nine interviewees, forty-seven were employed and, of these, twenty-two were working in regular full-time jobs, eight were self-employed, four were in full-time contractual work (*haken*), and thirteen worked part-time, the latter of which, however, in most cases meant a forty-hour work week. Typical occupations included clerical worker, elder care worker, school teacher, accountant, pharmacist, and public sector employee (particularly, school-kitchen worker), along with self-employed occupations of writer, artist, or owner or manager of a small store. Among those who were not employed (twelve), four were unemployed and in search of employment, two were attending school or further training, and six did not work for other reasons, often having to do with their health, a recent experience of domestic violence, the disability of a child, or other personal circumstances.

To be able to grasp the specific challenges of working motherhood, I also chose to focus particularly on mothers who were taking care of preschool-aged children at the time of the interview. In the second phase of my research (in 2004 and 2005), which took place five years later, I focused mostly on women in their early to late forties with children of school age, who were largely from the same generation as the previous group but whose children were by then older, allowing me to get a sense of the long-term experiences of single mothers who separated when their children were below school age. More specifically, at the time of the interviews, the youngest child of thirty-one mothers was below school age, thirteen had elementary school aged children, nine had high school aged children, and five had grown children. The focus on mothers of young children also meant that most were in a period of transition, having separated or divorced quite recently and in the course of trying to forge a new lifestyle as a single mother. In short, by focusing on mothers of preschoolers, the life stories of the women in this book shed light on a particularly difficult period in managing the work-life balance as a single mother.

Because mothers' age at the birth of their first child varied (from age 18 to 46), they do not represent women of a single generation. Most of the mothers were born in the 1950s (seventeen), 1960s (twenty-six), and early 1970s (eleven), while four were born before 1950. While mothers shared the particular experience of raising small children on their own, their attitudes and experiences were thus formed in different historical contexts particular to their generation. Whereas the generation of women born in the 1950s and early 1960s benefited from the expanding educational and employment opportunities of the period of high-speed growth and were from the first postwar generation to delay marriage, women born in the late 1960s and 1970s, who came of age during the Bubble economy, were the ones at the center of the crisis surrounding fertility following the so-called "1.57 shock" of 1989 (an announcement in June 1990 that Japan's fertility rate had declined to 1.57 children per woman in that year) and were young adults at the time the economic Bubble burst. As educational and employment opportunities differed sharply between the "pre-Bubble" generation of women born before 1960 and the later "Bubble" generation, the particular circumstances of their upbringing also need closer consideration.

There were, of course, also important differences among mothers in terms of educational attainment. Although the image of single mothers in the press often leaves the impression that single mothers are highly educated women who have benefited from access to education, career, and income, single mothers in Japan tend, on average, to be less educated than married women (Fujiwara 2005b). That is to say, highly educated single mothers are more visible, but they do not necessarily represent the majority of single mothers. In this study, I deliberately included junior college graduates (nine) and university graduates (twenty), as well as graduates of senior high schools (twenty-six) and four women who did not complete their high school degrees. Although university graduates are overrepresented, the voices of the women in this study capture a broad range of experiences of women of different socioeconomic backgrounds. As I will discuss further in the chapters that follow, class background not only influenced mothers' educational attainment, but also had an impact on their work opportunities, resources, and personal outlooks as single mothers.

My aim here, therefore, is to examine the unity as well as diversity of experiences of single mothers rather than to rely on a singular categorization based on marital status. As will become apparent from the chapters to follow, other dimensions of their social background, in particular their generational and class background, were often more influential in shaping their experiences and perspectives.

A note on names: I use pseudonyms in place of all names of interviewees, and have in some cases altered minor details to ensure their anonymity. In line with Japanese conventions, the names of interviewees and Japanese scholars are written surname first, except in the case of Japanese scholars who publish in English.

CHAPTER OUTLINE

The chapters of this book trace the class dimensions of postwar Japanese family life and single mothers' negotiations of their gender and class identities on several levels. Chapter 1 introduces readers to the main characteristics of the postwar Japanese family ideal and its implications for the life courses and living conditions of women and single mothers. The ideal of the salaryman and professional housewife, I argue, not only constitutes a hegemonic ideal that has been institutionalized through social policies and company practices, but also needs to be considered as a mechanism that has reinforced a gender division of labor in the family and workplace and has contributed to the differentiation and marginalization of single mothers within postwar Japanese society.

Chapter 2 and chapter 3 place the lived realities of this ideal in the context of the life stories of single mothers from the pre-Bubble and Bubble generations. Their stories of their childhood highlight the changing character of family life in early postwar Japan and how their personal experiences of family life informed their dispositions toward education, employment, marriage, and motherhood. The stories from the Bubble generation also reveal a standardized life course and normative family ideal as a central frame for these women's approaches to marriage and motherhood. The lifestyle of the married full-time housewife and mother, in this context, appears not only as a gender role but also as a means of confirming one's gender and class identities and as a symbol of social achievement and status.

Chapter 4 and chapter 5 turn to women's experiences in becoming single mothers. To shed light on this transition, chapter 4 examines the specific conditions that come to define women's circumstances as single mothers. The challenges and limits they face in supporting themselves and their children through employment highlight not only the difficulty of balancing work and family as a single parent, but also the impact of the gendered life course encouraged by social policies and company practices on their ability to form an autonomous household and support themselves and their children through income from work.

Going beyond women's material circumstances and employment, chapter 5 explores the class dimensions of women's negotiations of their identities as women and mothers. Based on mothers' narratives, I outline subtle differences in the ways in which mothers interpret the significance of their low income and manage the work-family balance in the setting of priorities between their children's needs and their performance at work and in their perspectives on "good mothering." Such differences in their reproductive strategies show that to achieve a middle-class upbringing for their children not only requires a certain amount of material resources, but also comes with a specific attitude and disposition toward their children's education and upbringing. In other words, the role of the full-time housewife and education mother is not just a middle-class ideal, but also constitutes a practice that potentially plays an important role in facilitating a child's future educational attainment and job prospects, particularly when faced with constrained resources. Mothers' reproductive practices, viewed from this perspective, are not just a reflection of general expectations toward women's role in the family, but also offer insight into class-specific practices and the reproduction of social class in contemporary Japan.

Chapter One

Single Mothers and the Postwar Japanese Family

One of the most iconic images of postwar Japanese family life is that of the salaryman and the full-time "professional" housewife. Since the 1960s, the salaryman and the professional housewife have had an ubiquitous and hegemonic presence in discussions of postwar family life (Goldstein-Gideoni 2012; Hendry 1993; Imamura 1987; Vogel 1963). What distinguished the lifestyle of the salaryman family when first described by Ezra Vogel's study (1963) from the 1960s was, however, not just its traditional division of labor, represented by a full-time housewife wholly dedicated to the household and children, but also the association of the salaryman and his family with modernity and affluence. Unlike shopkeepers and craftsmen involved in independent business, who faced fluctuations in business and long work hours, Vogel noted, the salaryman's lifestyle as an employee was associated with a remarkable stability. As an employee of a large company in the newly emerging sectors of the economy, the salaryman enjoyed a lifestyle with a regular salary and a predictable future, ensured by lifetime employment in a thriving postwar economy (ibid., 9).

The salaryman's lifestyle was also associated with the "New Bright Life" (*akarui seikatsu*), a level of affluence that signified a departure from the daily struggles experienced by many in the aftermath of the war. Ownership of modern household appliances and consumer electronics—"sacred treasures" such as televisions, washing machines, and refrigerators—became central indicators of the affluence and modernity of the postwar family (Partner 1999, 138). The postwar Japanese family ideal of the salaryman and the full-time housewife, therefore, needs to be considered not only as a normative ideal and yardstick that has defined family life and gender roles in postwar Japan (Goldstein-Gideoni 2012), but even more importantly as a class-specific lifestyle, which not only set a standard for material affluence but also defined the cultural expression of middle-class family life.

This chapter introduces the main characteristics of the postwar Japanese family ideal, from its ascribed features and reinforcement through policies and company practices to the gender and class dimensions of the ideal, which also inform the lifestyles and living conditions of single mothers. While the salaryman family ideal has surely not stood unquestioned (Roberson and Suzuki 2003; White 2002), it remains an important factor of influence on the lives of women growing up and coming of age in the post-World War II period. For single mothers, moreover, the normative presence of the postwar Japanese family ideal is not just a matter of personal attitudes but can also be considered a major mechanism that differentiates and marginalizes women who fail to conform to the ideal.

SALARYMEN AND PROFESSIONAL HOUSEWIVES

One of the most central features of the postwar Japanese family ideal is not only that it promoted a specific ideal of a family composed of a salaryman and full-time housewife and a gender division of labor, but, more importantly, that it upheld the role of the full-time housewife and mother as a model of modern womanhood, one that promised women a sense of status and achievement. Whereas young men in early postwar Japan aspired to become salarymen in a large company, women were expected to become their counterpart, the full-time "professional" housewife. "The young girl," Vogel observed in the 1960s, "hopes to marry a salary man even if his salary were lower because his life is steady, he has leisure time, and she can be free of the anxieties and work connected with independent business" (1963, 9). Marriage to a salaryman, in other words, came to be viewed as equivalent to lifetime employment and a middle-class status for women. Later studies have confirmed the prestige and status ascribed to the role of the full-time housewife. In her study from the early 1990s of professional housewives, Joy Hendry asserted: "Housework and the care of children has undoubtedly always been a part of the working life of Japanese women, as it is part of the lives of most women, but in few parts of the world have these roles been granted the importance and status they have acquired in Japan" (1993, 224). Even for working women, according to some observers, the role of the housewife and mother remains one of the most central sources of their identity (Leblanc 1999, 31). Furthermore, recent studies underline the continuing prominence of motherhood as an ideal, a source of identity, and a practice (Holloway 2010).

Central to the ideal of the professional housewife and mother is, however, not just her presence in the home but a specific culture of mothering, a culture heavily invested in facilitating an offspring's upbringing and future career (Vogel 1978; White 1987). Mothering, in this case, is not just about domesticity, but also serves to symbolically represent and reinforce a certain class status. Mothers play a central role in supporting their children during high school and university exams. They foster their children's academic performance by cooking nutritious meals, fixing late night snacks, and ensuring that children do not forget any important school items (Imamura 1987, 20). Mothers' investment in children's education, moreover, has developed to such an extent that childhood in Japan has become modeled on work life, demanding diligence, productivity, and long hours of study from children from a young age, in order to ensure entry into a privileged school or university (Field 1995). Also called "education mothers" (*kyôiku mama*), dedicated mothers have made ensuring their children's educational success and future career into their full-time job (Imamura 1987). The activities of middle-class professional housewives and mothers are thus not just reflective of mothers' investment in their children's upbringing, but can also be considered a specific cultural practice and class culture, aimed at ensuring their children's middle-class future.

As studies of company policies have shown, housewives have also played an instrumental role in supporting the work and lifestyle of their salaryman husband. In taking care of household matters, including activities such as the selection of schools for children or purchase of a house or apartment, housewives allow men to work long hours and fully dedicate themselves to their companies (Allison 1994). In Yuko Ogasawara's study of Office Ladies (1998), it is the wives of salarymen who smoothe work relations by making sure their husbands provide appropriate gifts to secretaries. Some companies even introduced campaigns to train wives of company employees in household management and child-rearing (Gordon 1997), highlighting the integral role played by housewives in supporting the existence and success of large corporations.

Housewives are also known to be involved in activities not strictly confined to the home, which underscores the publicly recognized nature of the role and responsibilities attributed to married housewives. While housework and childcare is always the first priority, outside activities that do not interfere with domestic duties, such as part-time work or volunteer activities, are not unusual. Women's outside activities and their relationship to their identity as a housewife can be illustrated by the contributions made by environmental and consumer groups largely composed of housewives (Gelb and Estevez-Abe 1998; Hendry 1993; Leblanc 1999). For example, the Seikatsu Club, a consumer cooperative born out of the concerns of a group of housewives over rising milk prices, selects products meeting standards of safety and quality and delivers them to members at reasonable prices. Today, the Seikatsu Club is a nationwide network that delivers groceries to the doorstep and supports housewife representatives at running for political office in local assemblies. Even though prices of consumer goods and local politics and regulations are public policy issues, women's involvement in these issues does not seem to contradict the domestic role of the professional housewife. Taking responsibility of the home, in this case, not only means performing housework and childcare in the privacy of the home, but also justifies public activities concerned with the welfare of the family and community (Leblanc 1999).

To be a housewife in Japan, then, carries important responsibilities and a broader role in society, the economy, and the state. Housewives' dedication to the well-being of their families and their devotion to the educational success of their children has meant that the role of the full-time housewife has been widely described not simply as a gender role, but also as a profession, a lifelong career, and a sign of status matching that of her professional, white-collar husband (Hendry 1993; Imamura 1987; Vogel 1978). Women may thus aspire to be housewives not simply because of a preoccupation with femininity and domesticity, but rather more because of the prestige and social status conferred. Just as marriage to a salaryman and the role of the professional housewife is a sign of social status, so is children's educational attainment a central ingredient for confirming that status. Motherhood, in this context, does not merely constitute a practice of nurturing and child-rearing, but also comes with a specific lifestyle and purpose, aimed at ensuring children's educational success and future middle-class status.

The privilege associated with being a professional housewife is also underscored by the fact that becoming a full-time homemaker has long been a predominantly middle-class phenomenon. In the 1950s, when the role of the professional housewife began to enter public discourse, full-time housewives constituted only a minority among married women (Partner 1999, 152). Although their number increased during the years of high economic growth and peaked in the late 1960s and 1970s, full-time housewives have never accounted for more than 38% of married women and can be estimated to be largely accounted for by families of salaried husbands in management positions in large companies (Osawa 2002, 260). The widespread availability of public day care centers—which, unlike kindergartens, provide full-day care for children of working mothers—instead indicates that full-time work among married mothers is not uncommon in Japan. Whereas middle-class women have been encouraged to become professional housewives, working-class women whose husband's income falls below a certain threshold have continued to work even when taking care of small children (Fuse 1984; Kamata 1987).

These class aspects of the housewife ideal are also highlighted by studies of working-class mothers, which present a more critical stance toward the role of the full-time housewife. Glenda S. Roberts (1994), in her study from the 1990s, notes that most of the blue-collar women she interviewed worked for economic reasons—to keep up with rising living standards and to pay for consumer goods associated with the lifestyle of the new middle-class, such as refrigerators, cars, and cram school attendance to ensure entry into a prestigious high school. While the working-class women she interviewed aspired to a middle-class living standard, Roberts also observes that they rejected the role of the full-time housewife as an "easy lifestyle" that comes with "three meals and a nap" and as boring, snobbish, and narrowly focused on household matters and television-watching (ibid., 30). In Dorinne Kondo's research, working-class women also voice their resistance to "pushing their children to study" and instead emphasize their commitment to working outside of the home as a reflection of their dedication as mothers to their families and their children's welfare (1990, 285). Dispositions and practices toward mothering and education, therefore, are not singular but can differ along class lines.

Class differences in the living conditions of families and their impact on children's educational trajectories have also been documented in a number of studies. Yoshiyuki Kudomi's (1993) pioneering study of a low-income family housing complex has shown that parents in low-income households, including single-mother households, do not lack ambitions for their children's education and future, but face considerable constraints in their living conditions, making it difficult to invest more time and energy in their children's future. Underscoring existing disparities in children's educational experience depending on social background, Yuma Konishi's research (2003) on families receiving public assistance has also shown that children from low-income families are more likely to skip school, are less likely to attend cram schools, achieve lower scores at school, and have fewer friends. Takehiko Kariya's research has further highlighted disparities in children's academic skills and scholastic performance depending on family environment, which is also reflected in differences in cultural capital (2001; 2010).

Social class, in the context of family life, is thus not just a matter of economics, but is also expressed in different living conditions, family lifestyles, and approaches to parenting and educational attainment. More specifically, Yuki Honda (2004) has shown that, since the 1990s, mothers from a lower-class background and with a low educational attainment have shown decreasing ambition to become an "education mother," contributing to the widening of class differences in adherence to this ideal. Even if mothers have an ambition for their children to excel in school, the lack of time and cultural resources hampers their efforts. A study of families in disadvantaged communities in Buraku districts also shows that families often lack the knowledge and cultural capital to support their children's schooling, despite their best intentions (Kanbara 2000b). Yutaka Hasegawa's (2014) recent study has further confirmed the contemporary relevance of these conclusions. In his study, low-income families had ambitions for their children's future but did not pursue the same parenting strategies as middle-class families. Aware that higher educational attainment was not affordable even if their children excelled in school, parents instead tried to mitigate their children's sense of disadvantage by encouraging them to take pride in their completion of a high school degree and their early economic independence.

The middle-classness of the salaryman family is, therefore, not only expressed by the material affluence of the salaryman family's lifestyle, visualized in the possession of coveted consumer appliances, children's cram school attendance, and the presence of a stay-at-home mother and housewife, all supported by the salaryman's family wage. Middle-class family lifestyles also foster children's cultural capital and educational future by investing in specific educational and cultural activities and through mothers' close engagement with their children's educational development. Differences in material and living conditions, therefore, not only are expressed by levels of consumption, but also contribute to lifestyles and parenting practices, which may affect children's cultural capital and educational future.

THE POSTWAR JAPANESE FAMILY SYSTEM

The salaryman family and professional housewife ideal, however, do not just represent a specific social aspiration and lifestyle; as a lifestyle supported by a range of government policies and regulations, the ideal can also be considered as a stratifying mechanism that reinforces gender and class distinctions in Japanese society. As Fumino Yokoyama's (2002) detailed analysis has shown, from family law, education, and taxation to labor law and childcare services, policies and regulations in postwar Japan have presumed and reinforced a specific model of family, that of a salaried husband and full-time housewife. In the 1960s, education promoted a gender division of labor through compulsory school subjects such as home economics for girls. Lack of investment in day care services, as well as the provision of maternity leave, further made childcare a private matter and the responsibility of women and families. Pension and tax schemes did not explicitly use the family as a unit, but did provide incentives for women to limit their work activities and income in order to maintain their eligibility for tax deductions for dependent spouses and to avoid payment of pension contributions (Osawa 2002). Described as the Postwar Japanese Family System (Ochiai 1994), such policies encouraged women to become housewives during a period that was assumed to provide greater opportunities to women.

Although women's educational attainment increased, the tendency for women to become professional housewives and remain dependent on their husbands intensified during the 1960s and 1970s. Most strikingly, women with university degrees were, until the 1980s, less likely to be engaged in paid work than were high school graduates (Brinton 1993). Women university graduates not only had difficulties in finding a job because of overqualification for clerical jobs, to which women were often assigned, but they also were encouraged to become professional housewives because of the middle-class status of their husbands (Ogasawara 1998).

By the 1980s, the difficulty in pursuing equal employment opportunities despite women's increasing educational attainment generated contradictions and conflicts but was met with a conservative assertion of a "Japanese-style welfare society" (cf. Takahashi 1997; White and Goodman 1998). Despite increasing need for public day care facilities, government policies continued to assume that children would be taken care of within the family. In the long term, this not only made it difficult for women who were mothers to work, but also increased the costs of having children, with the consequence of delayed childbirth and lower fertility (Shimoebisu 1994). Moreover, the policy emphasis shifted from the family as "target" of social support to the family as pillar and source of welfare in Japanese society (Harada 1988). That is, not only did women receive little support in balancing work and family, their unpaid labor in taking care of children and the elderly became a constitutive element of Japan's welfare regime (Esping-Andersen 1999; Yokoyama 2002). The salaryman family, viewed from this perspective, was not merely a social ideal generated by the changing family lifestyles of the period of rapid economic expansion but also should be considered a consequence of government policies that considered women's care for husbands, children, and the elderly a key element of the Japanese economy and welfare state.

The model of family promoted by social policies also supported what has been called a "corporate centered society" (Fujii 2002; Kimoto 1995). As Mari Osawa (1993) argued, social policies in Japan have promoted the role of the male breadwinner employed at a large corporation as the standard, while marginalizing those who do not adhere to this ideal. In addition to assuming that women would become housewives and dependents, policies have focused on the job security and high living standards of male employees of large corporations, who constitute a minority among Japanese workers. Low-income families with a breadwinner employed at a smaller company or in a family business, by contrast, have received very limited support. Whereas employees in large corporations can benefit from a seniority system and ample company family allowances, workers in small and medium-sized companies do not enjoy the same job security and benefits. Moreover, state support in the form of a child allowance has been introduced very late and has only recently been expanded, highlighting the very limited support offered to low-income families (Oshio 1996). Such policy preferences make the life of the salaryman appealing not only because of its association with modernity and affluence, but also because of the benefits and material underpinnings attached to his employment at a large company and his middle-class status.

Beyond government policies, large corporations such as Matsushita or Toyota, which were at the center of the high-speed growth economy of the 1960s, also played a role in reinforcing a specific type of family that maximized productivity and encouraged consumption. Companies were cognizant of the fact that professional housewives played an important role in providing a family environment where hardworking husbands could rest, relax, and physically and psychologically recuperate from a long workday and where they could gather strength and motivation for the next day of work (Meguro and Shibata 1999). In other words, not only were company employees expected to show their loyalty and to dedicate their lives to their companies (Rohlen 1974), employees' families as a whole were mobilized to commit themselves to the growth and prosperity of the company. The ideal family, in this context, was oriented to the material underpinnings of family life: a hardworking husband with a stable income who can pay for a family home and a family car (Kimoto 2000).

Companies have also reinforced women's domesticity with a persistent gender division of labor in the workplace, which has limited women's opportunities to become economically independent and to choose a lifestyle outside of the male-breadwinner family. The introduction of a family wage, lifetime employment, and the seniority system assured the worker of his ability to sustain himself and his family, but also marginalized women, leading to the persistent gender gap in wages, as well as diminishing women's work opportunities and ability to earn a living wage (Kimoto 2000). The distinction between permanent employees with lifetime employment (*seishain*) and non-permanent employees in contractual or part-time positions, in particular, has led to the gender segregation of the labor market and a decrease in women's employment opportunities (Osawa 1999). Companies invest in young employees with an outlook for long-term employment, but are hesitant to do so in the case of women, who are likely to quit upon marriage and childbirth. As a consequence, women have long been placed in clerical positions with no outlook for promotion, as a type of reserve army of labor (Brinton 1993; 2001).

Until the introduction of the Equal Employment Opportunities Law, women were usually only offered monotonous clerical jobs with no opportunity of advancement and encouraged to quit their jobs upon marriage. The lack of challenges, promotion, and recognition on the job, as well as low remuneration, not only have limited women's economic independence but also have made the role of the housewife a more appealing means to some women for achieving a middle-class living standard and recognition for their abilities and achievements (Ogasawara 1998). Although women have recently begun to enter career-track positions in greater numbers, only a few pursue this option, as it remains difficult to balance work and family (Rosenbluth 2007). Gender roles and family lifestyles in postwar Japan have, therefore, not been an inevitable outcome of "traditions"—real or invented—but can also be considered an integral element of Japan's corporate society and welfare state regime.

GENDERED LIFE COURSES

Needless to say, the prescriptions and reinforcement of specific gendered lifestyles by the Postwar Japanese Family System have also had wide-ranging implications for women's lives. Trends in marriage, childbirth, and women's employment, as well as attitudinal studies, highlight the growing contradictions women have come to face in weighing their options of marriage, motherhood, and employment in the postwar economy and society.

On the one hand, women's life courses in postwar Japan have been highly predictable: the timing of marriage and childbirth have been heavily clustered within a narrow age range, and the subsequent withdrawal from the workforce has long been a persistent pattern (Brinton 1992; 1993; Iwai and Manabe 2000). On the other hand, trends in marriage and childbirth also highlight growing hesitation about a predictable life course of tying the knot and having a family. The average age at first marriage has increased from 26.6 years for men and 23.8 years for women in 1955 to 30.5 years and 28.8 years, respectively, in 2010 (IPSS 2012). While this does not mean the rejection of marriage as a possibility, the number of men and women who have remained unmarried for life has more than doubled since 1995, reaching 20.14% for men and 10.61% for women in 2010 (ibid.). This trend has also been paralleled by a marked decline in fertility. Since the "1.57 shock," the trend toward fewer children (*shôshika*) has become a serious social and policy concern (Jolivet 1997; Tendo 2003). Although there has been a moderate improvement in the fertility rate since 2005, when it reached a historical low of 1.26, Japan's fertility rate to date remains well below the population replacement level (MHLW 2013b). The decline in the average number of children per woman does, however, not mean that most families in Japan have only one child. Family size, in fact, remains at an average of two children per family, as in addition to a decline in marriage the growing presence of childless married couples has also contributed to an overall decline in fertility levels (Higuchi and Ota 2004; Shirahase 2010).

To explain the growing hesitance surrounding marriage and childbirth, we also need to take a closer look at the changing meanings associated with marriage and having a family. The survey on "Attitudes toward Marriage and the Family among Japanese Singles," conducted by the National Institute of

Population and Social Security Research since 1987 (IPSS 2010), offers important insights here. Although love marriage has clearly replaced arranged marriages in the postwar period, women's response to the question of whether they think it is more crucial "to get married by a specific age" or whether they would rather "wait until the perfect partner is found," has been wavering. Between 1987 and 2002, waiting for the perfect partner garnered a majority, but this trend has reversed since then (ibid., 2). Age of course also plays a role. Even if the majority of women in their early twenties (60%) indicate that they are not in a hurry to get married, women between thirty and thirty-four do so to a much lesser extent (13%; ibid., 3). While marriage to a partner of choice remains the ideal, the timing of marriage remains a central source of pressure and a driving force behind women's approaches to marriage.

Marriage also remains strongly associated with family formation. When asked about the "benefits" of marriage, the "ability to have children" ranks by far as the most important factor for women, followed by the ability to achieve "a sense of stability" through marriage. "The ability to live with someone one loves," notably, ranks only in fourth place, with less than half the responses of "the ability to have children" (IPSS 2010, 5). Even if a love marriage is taken for granted, therefore, motherhood remains the most central element of women's understandings of marriage (Kamano 2004b). Research has shown that married women see themselves primarily as mothers, rather than as wives (Yazawa, Kunihiro, and Tendo 2003), suggesting that motherhood remains, even now, a powerful source of their self-identity and motivation to marry.

Yet the high status attributed to motherhood also has its downsides. Asked about the major "cost" of marriage, women cite the "loss of freedom in one's personal conduct and lifestyle," imposed by the expectation to become a mother and housewife once married, as a major factor (Ehara 2004; IPSS 2010; Kamano 2004a). That is, while motherhood remains an important source of personal accomplishment and public recognition, women's knowledge of the high expectations faced by housewives and mothers also makes them associate marriage with personal constraint. Many mothers, therefore, find themselves in a double bind. On the one hand, they continue to emphasize the importance of being a mother and raising children on their own. On the other hand, they also wish to find sources of self-fulfillment outside of child-rearing, which is, however, difficult given the demands of full-time motherhood (Ehara 2000).

This difficulty of combining work and marriage is a central issue that also heavily affects women's views of marriage and their life course (Fuwa 2013; Nemoto 2008; Raymo and Iwasawa 2005). Since the 1990s, the aspiration of becoming a full-time housewife has consistently declined among single women and both men and women increasingly highlight their goal of continuing to work after marriage and childbirth (IPSS 2010, 11). However, when asked about their planned life course, there is a noticeable difference between ideal and expected reality. While a growing number of women hope to continue working while having a family (30.6%) or to interrupt and then return to work (35.2%), rather than to become a full-time housewife (19.7%), in real terms only 9.1% expect to become a full-time housewife and fewer women who would like to be able to balance work and family expect to be able to do so (24.7%), instead planning to interrupt work with marriage and childbirth (36.1%; ibid.). In other words, not only do women express doubts that balancing work and family will, indeed, be possible; even those who hope to become housewives realize that they may actually not be able to do so in practice.

Remaining single also comes with major challenges. Chided as "parasite singles," working singles residing with their parents have been accused of enjoying an easy lifestyle in evading marriage and benefitting from a large disposable income by saving on rent and everyday expenses, which they may then spend on designer handbags and foreign travel (Yamada 1999). Empirical data has, however, shown that singles residing with family do contribute to the family income and that single women who live by themselves lead frugal lifestyles, indicating the continuing difficulty for women to make ends meet on their own (Higuchi and Ota 2004). Raymo and Ono (2007), moreover, find that while single women who reside with their family may assume fewer domestic responsibilities, there is little evidence to support the "parasite single" thesis. While women may not feel immediate pressure to marry for economic reasons, there is little support for the assumption that women have become more independent from marriage and family support, despite their increased engagement in work.

Yet, precisely because women hope to find a partner with a stable income, someone who can support a wife and children, finding a suitable partner is becoming increasingly difficult. Delays in marriage, as Raymo and Ishikawa (2005) have shown, may have more to do with changes in the marriage market, that is, with the limited availability of highly educated husbands earning a good salary, than with women's economic independence. Since women are expected to make big sacrifices and be dedicated homemakers, they, in turn, wish at least for a "good marriage" to a husband with a high and stable income (Ehara 1994). Yet, the recession, a general decline in lifetime employment, and increasing youth unemployment also make it increasingly difficult for young men to offer the stability and affluent lifestyle of the typical postwar middle-class marriage. For the majority of women who lived with their parents when single, marriage is actually likely to constitute a decline in living standards, since a young husband's salary is often lower than that of a wife's father (Yamada 2000). As marriage continues to be considered a source of economic security and upward mobility, it is men with lower educational attainment and low earning potential who are the ones facing the greatest difficulties in finding a partner (Shirahase 2010). In short, women not only struggle with limited opportunities to become economically independent and pursue alternative lifestyles, but also with the decrease of the idealized salaryman husband who provides a stable income and high social status.

Contemporary aspirations of marriage and family, viewed from this perspective, reflect a complex dialectic between aspirations toward motherhood and marriage as a source of stability and status and concerns about the pressures and constraints associated with getting married and becoming a mother. While women have gained opportunities in education and employment and are increasingly ambitious about combining work and family, there is also a persistent concern over the fact that balancing work and family remains difficult and, moreover, that reliance on husbands as the sole breadwinners is becoming increasingly unfeasible. Women's perspectives on marriage and family, therefore, reflect both the continuing salience of the normative family ideal in women's views of marriage and family and the growing friction surrounding an ideal that is increasingly difficult to realize in practice.

MOTHERHOOD AND SOCIAL POLICY

In light of the challenges and constraints associated with marriage and motherhood, single mothers are often considered to be women who have chosen to pursue a lifestyle outside of the normative ideal of the married wife and mother, a choice fostered by women's economic independence. As we have seen, however, there is little evidence to support the thesis that single women have grown more economically independent from marriage and family. Statistics on single mothers further support this view. Divorce is considerably more prevalent among women with lower educational attainment, i.e., those without a university degree (Fujiwara 2005b), and among women who are least likely to be able to make ends meet on their own (Ono 2010; Raymo, Iwasawa, and Bumpass 2004). Single mothers are not only considerably more likely to rely on public assistance than are heads of other types of households (16.2% as opposed to 6.6% in 2011; MHLW 2012b), but reliance on public assistance among single mothers has also been increasing in past decades. The socioeconomic origins of single mothers, their reliance on public assistance, and the generally high poverty rate of single mothers (Abe 2014) instead highlight the very limits of women's economic independence and the repercussions of pursuing a lifestyle outside of the married-mother norm.

To be sure, single mothers have received government assistance in various forms, particularly when compared to other types of individuals and households in need, most especially compared to single fathers (Kasuga 1989; Nakada, Sugimoto, and Morita 2001) and single men (Gill 2011). Characteristic of single-mother policies in Japan is, however, that while policies have offered special protection for them as mothers with dependent children, in contrast to the treatment of middle-class housewives, single mothers have actually received very little support for their role as mothers. In other words, while single-mother policies have played an important role in supporting the living conditions of single mothers and their children, they have also contributed to the differentiation and stratification of family lifestyles.

The centerpiece of single-mother policies in postwar Japan to date is the dependent children's allowance (*jidô fuyô teate*), which remains the most central source of support for the majority of single mothers. Conceived as an alternative to livelihood support in the form of public assistance, the dependent children's allowance entitles single mothers to support on the basis of their status as a single mother head-of-household (and, therefore, does not carry the same stigma as does public assistance) and supports single mothers without an independent income as well as working single mothers with a moderate income. More specifically, as of 2008, single mothers with an annual income below ¥1.3 million (US$11,818) were eligible for the full amount of ¥41,720 (US$379) per month for the first child, which was reduced on a sliding scale to ¥9,850 (US$90) per month for those earning up to ¥3.65 million per year (US$33,182, MHLW 2008). Since single mothers' average annual income remains ¥2.43 million (US$22,090 in 2012, MHLW 2013a), the allowance has in many cases constituted a central addition to these mothers' low, and often unstable, wages.

In addition to cash assistance, single mothers have also received other forms of support, which have helped reduce their daily expenses. As low-income families and single mothers, they can apply for public housing apartments, which considerably reduce their housing expenses. In 2010, 18.1% of single mothers lived in public housing units (MHLW 2011). There are also special subsidized apartments set aside for single mothers (*boshi apâto*) and dormitories for single mothers (*boshi seikatsu shien shisetsu*), the latter in which single mothers are also offered consultations and other services. Like other citizens and residents, single mothers are also covered by the national health insurance scheme (*kokumin kenkô hoken*), and low-income mothers are eligible for waivers of co-payments in some localities. Most importantly, single mothers have had access to publicly subsidized public day care services, the costs of which are reduced or waived for low-income single-mother households. Although metropolitan areas are particularly known to have long waiting lists for places in day care centers, single mothers are given preferential treatment in obtaining a place for their children and 61.8% of single mothers rely on day care centers for their children's care. Even if mothers are residing with their parents, few rely on parents (4.3%) or family (0.7%) for their children's care (MHLW 2011).

Defined as a group that is "hard to employ," single mothers have also benefited from access to a range of employment-related services, as well as from special measures aimed at supporting single mothers' ability to improve their vocational skills. In addition to a low- or no-interest loan program (*boshi fukushi shikin*) to support vocational training, the establishment of a small business, or children's education, single mothers also have access to job centers (*kôkyô shokugyô anteijô* or *harô wâku*) that provide information on job openings as well as consultations. Single mothers are also offered special vocational training programs and subsidies to pursue vocational qualifications (such as clerical accounting or elder care) to support their ability to reenter the job market after marriage, childbirth, and divorce.

While few would doubt the potential benefits of measures supporting single mothers' employment and independent income, the enforcement of working motherhood among single mothers also stands in sharp contrast to policies that have promoted the role of the full-time housewife among married middle-class mothers. Whereas middle-class mothers have been encouraged to minimize their employment, policies regarding single mothers have from their inception in early postwar Japan taken for granted that these women would work full-time (Fujiwara 2005a; Peng 1997). Rather than supporting stay-at-home motherhood as a universal value, postwar policies have differentiated the needs of mothers based not only on their social class but also on their marital status.

Similarly, while middle-class mothers have been encouraged to rely on a male breadwinner for their own and their children's welfare, the same paternal responsibility has not been enforced in the case of single mothers. Although child support payments by fathers are required by the Civil Code, to date child support payments remain poorly enforced (Shimoebisu 2008). Although welfare reforms have tried to promote greater enforcement, in the latest national survey on single mothers only 19.7% report receiving child support payments, even though 37.7% had oral or written agreements on child support payments (MHLW 2011). Because almost 90% of divorces in Japan are completed based on "mutual agreement" (*kyôgi rikon*), that is, without going through the court system, few couples determine child support payments. Agreements on child support, and actual reception of payments, also tend to be more prevalent among university graduates with higher incomes than among those with high school education and the greatest financial needs (MHLW 2011, 7). Even in cases of a judicial divorce, however, child support payments remain difficult to enforce, highlighting the low priority given to children's rights (Shimoebisu 2008) and to paternal responsibility for their welfare in the case of single mothers.

Instead, a considerable share of single mothers relies on parents in managing everyday life. As much as a quarter of single mothers reside with parents or family, particularly when their children are small (Abe 2005). While co-residence appears to ease the work-family balance, it does not actually eliminate single mothers' need to earn an income (Abe and Oishi 2005; Raymo and Zhou 2012). In fact, single mothers who reside with their parents are more likely to work longer hours and spend less time with their children (Raymo et al. 2014). The ability to rely on family is, moreover, not equally available to single mothers: single mothers with a lower educational attainment have been found to be able to rely considerably less on their family for material or informal support (Iwata 2004).

But even if single mothers do their best to support themselves through employment, there are clear limits on their ability to become economically independent through work, as envisioned by policymakers. On the one hand, single mothers are more likely to work full-time and in permanent positions compared to married mothers (50.3% as opposed to 32.5% in 1997; JIL 2003, 182). Yet, working full-time and achieving a permanent position when children are small remains difficult. Among married mothers, the ratio working in permanent positions is 56.1% at the time of their child's birth, after which it falls to 26.9% and recovers to 31.6% by the time children complete high school. In the case of single mothers, permanent employment is low for those with infants (27.4%), but rises to 47.0% for children aged six to eight years old and reaches 56.3% for those with children about to complete high school (ibid., 139).

This difficulty in obtaining a permanent position when children are below school age, moreover, has long-term consequences for single mothers' work status and income. Although permanent positions generally provide more job security and a higher income, incomes vary significantly depending on the length of job tenure as well as on age at entry into a permanent position. Whereas mothers who entered permanent positions below the age of twenty-seven earn incomes as high as ¥4.6 million (US$41,818) after age forty, those who enter such positions after the age of twenty-eight are unlikely to reach an income of ¥3.0 million (US$27,272, JIL 2003, 251). As the average age at first marriage is 26.8 (in 2000), and mothers' average age at first child's birth is 29.6 (MHLW 2004), mothers who attempt to enter permanent employment after becoming single mothers are likely already to be in their thirties. Since most women quit their jobs after giving birth and finding full-time, permanent employment while taking care of a toddler is difficult, a mother may not pursue permanent employment before her mid-thirties, which means that she might, according to available data (JIL 2003), at best earn between ¥1.8 and ¥2.6 million (US$16,363–23,636) even if she finds a permanent position. Part-time work, in turn, does not come with significant pay increases and part-time working single mothers' average income remains at just above ¥1.0 million (US$9,090) regardless of age and experience (ibid., 244).

There are also important differences in single mothers' income depending on their educational attainment. As Fujiwara (2005b) has shown, single mothers who are university and junior college graduates are more likely to hold permanent positions (51.8% and 38.7%, respectively) as compared to junior and senior high school graduates (23.5% and 28.0%, respectively). When viewed in terms of income, university-educated single mothers in permanent positions earn on average ¥4.6 million (US$41,818), while junior and senior high school graduates earn, respectively, only ¥2.5 and ¥2.9 million (US$22,727 and $26,363). In other words, even if a mother manages to obtain a permanent position at a fairly young age, a lower educational attainment means she would still be unlikely to reach an income above the income limit for the dependent children's allowance and to reach a level of income sufficient to make ends meet on her own.

The postwar ideal of the salaryman and the full-time or professional housewife, viewed from this perspective, constitutes not merely a social ideal, but can also be considered a source of class and gender stratification in postwar Japanese family life. The promotion of a male-breadwinner model of family through government policies and company practices, not only privileges middle-class housewives at a time when an increasing number of women wish and need to combine work and family and fewer men are able to find stable employment, but it also constitutes a source of differentiation of families and mothers who do not adhere to this ideal. Social policies have fostered not just stay-at-home motherhood but, more precisely, the stay-at-home motherhood of married middle-class mothers. Yet, full-time maternal care for children is a privilege of the few, and families with a lower household income and that are headed by single mothers do not receive the same support for the woman's role as a mother. While single mothers' ability to work as mothers may appear at first sight as a step toward independence, their low incomes and struggles to make ends meet also illustrate both their differentiation from a middle-class lifestyle and the disadvantages they face based on their marital status.

Chapter Two

Educational Pioneers

Kamata Toshiko was in her late forties when I first met her. Having grown up in a three-generation family running a family business in the 1950s, Kamata possesses a personal story that provides a close-up view of the wide-ranging social and economic changes that shaped the lives of Japanese women of her generation. Kamata's family owned a kimono business in a small town in western Japan. However, with the growth of the postwar economy and a shift to white-collar office jobs, Western-style clothing rapidly began to replace the traditional Japanese wardrobe. As a result, the business faltered, which was followed by her father's desertion of the family. Kamata credits her mother's perseverance for rebuilding the family business, transforming it into a bicycle repair store, which gave rise to a very different type of lifestyle while offering a stable income.

Interested in literature, Kamata enjoyed school, and without being able to articulate why, felt a strong urge upon graduation from high school to leave the countryside. She became the first in her family to obtain a university degree, thanks to the improved family finances. Her attendance of university in the late 1960s was an eye-opening experience, as it coincided with the period of nationwide student protests. She reflects: "I had come to the city from the countryside, where everything was according to the rules…. I had felt suffocated. [At the university, however,] it was a time when people started to say that the world can't stay like this, and that something has to be done." Kamata did not personally get involved with the student movement as she felt quite intimidated by their assertive views, but her university experience clearly left a mark on her vision of her personal future.

Upon graduation, Kamata struggled to find employment, as there were few job openings for female university graduates at the time, and she worked in various professions wherever opportunities arose. Quiet in disposition and modest in her personal ambitions, she had no particular career ambitions or confidence that she would enjoy or excel in a particular job. She explains: "Maybe it's just my personality, but for me, it is rather a question of whether I am able to do [a specific job]. If you keep doing something, you will develop the needed skills, right? Unless it is a very special job, everyone is the same, that is what I thought." Over time, she however gradually grew more self-confident, and when faced with a layoff, decided to become an active member of the union, which inspired her to become more assertive and actively work for the protection of her own and her co-workers' rights. Most central to Kamata's life story was her pioneering experience as a working single woman with a university degree. Invested in unionism, she had never considered marriage or motherhood as a personal goal. Yet, when faced with an unplanned pregnancy and a partner unwilling to recognize his child, Kamata—in keeping with her previous experience in uncharted territory—decided to forge ahead against the odds.

The image of single mothers in Japanese popular discourse often suggests that a single mother is a particular "type" of woman, one whose attitudes and values lead her to pursue a life course outside of the normative family ideal. Yet, as we see in Kamata's story, becoming a single mother is often far from the single mother's personal ambition. To be sure, Kamata stands out for her early urge to become independent from her family, her embrace of the critical stance taken by student movements and unionism, and her lack of enthusiasm for marriage and motherhood. However, even if her views are those of a minority, they are shared by many women of her generation and were hardly determinative of the fact that she would become a single mother. Rather, her understanding and approach to life highlight the specific socioeconomic conditions of her time, which shook up family life and gender roles and forced her and other women of her generation to embrace change and innovation and to engage with the newly emerging opportunities in education and employment. Single mothers, viewed from this perspective, are not single mothers a priori; instead, their experiences and life trajectories need to be examined within the specific social, structural, and historical circumstances of their time. Kamata's story, in this respect, is not just the personal story of a woman who became a single mother; it also offers a unique glimpse of the characteristic circumstances of the coming of age of women of her generation. How did the rapid expansion and modernization of the economy in the early post-World War II period impact the lives of women of this generation? What did it mean for women who grew up in the early postwar period to pursue an education, to work, and to marry?

In this chapter, I introduce the stories of Japanese single mothers from the pre-Bubble generation, women who, born in the 1950s, were among the first to benefit from greater educational opportunities to obtain a high school or university degree but also were among the first to delay marriage and motherhood. Their narratives of growing up during a period of rapid social and economic change are not presented simply to outline their personal upbringing and attitudes but, more importantly, to offer insight into their understanding of social status and social achievement and of the relationship of these to marriage and motherhood at a time of rapid social and economic change.

PATHWAYS TO EDUCATION

One of the central elements of the life stories of women born in the 1950s is that their family experiences took shape during a period of tremendous social and economic change (Gordon 2003; Ishida 2010). Changes in class structure, educational attainment, and employment not only opened up new opportunities; they also left a distinctive imprint on family life and individual life trajectories. Japanese middle-class families in the 1960s became less likely to own a business or farm and were more commonly headed by a salaryman in an office job, which, as described in detail by Ezra Vogel's study *Japan's New Middle Class* (1963), fundamentally altered the rhythm and lifestyle of postwar Japanese family life.

In addition, educational attainment grew exponentially, opening up to young people new opportunities that were not available to their parents. Whereas in 1960 just about half of men and women attended high school, by 1975 high school attendance had become almost universal. Similarly, a university education was rare for women in 1960, when only 5.5% of women (as opposed to 14.9% of men) enrolled in junior college or university. By the 1980s, however, tertiary education had become much more of a mass phenomenon, even if gender differences persisted: 33.3% of women enrolled in university or junior college, as opposed to 41.3% of men (MEXT 2006). The growth of educational attainment not only generated new prospects for the next generation, but also altered the meaning of education, as it shifted from an elite experience to a mass phenomenon.

Higher educational attainment also led to changes in women's employment patterns. Until the 1970s, employment was most common among female high school graduates, while few women university graduates proceeded into the labor force. By the 1980s, however, this relationship was reversed: more and more women university graduates sought employment after graduation, while female high school graduates entered the labor force in decreasing numbers (Brinton 1993, 40). The introduction of the Equal Employment Opportunities Law in 1986, moreover, promised women, legally at least, equal opportunities in entering the work force. Needless to say, these changing circumstances also constituted distinctive conditions, forming new outlooks and personal dispositions in relation to education, employment, and individual futures, and generating important differences between the pre-Bubble and Bubble generations.

Changes in the occupational structure in the decades following the end of the war also meant that the occupation and lifestyle of the father of a woman born in the 1950s were not necessarily a clear predictor of his child's future lifestyle. The "pre-Bubble" generation was raised by a generation of fathers and mothers who had experienced World War II and had grown up during the period of wartime losses and postwar rebuilding. Their childhoods preceded the stable, predictable life course associated with the so-called Postwar Japanese Family System (Ochiai 1994). Instead, their stories of growing up in the early postwar period expressed a vision of the future that was filled with promise and opportunity for those who dared to take initiative. Their fathers were largely born in the first decade of the Showa period (the so-called *showa hitoketa* generation) and are widely considered a generation that built successful and independent careers in a period of tremendous socio-economic change. Open to innovation and change, they took advantage of expanding economic opportunities and successfully built businesses or small to medium-sized factories employing new technologies. Their life courses reflected the entrepreneurial spirit of the postwar period as well as the real opportunities for social mobility that were available. As a consequence, women's own understanding of class and social mobility was also not necessarily focused on access to assets and economic capital, but more often on the meritocratic opportunities of a democratic society and the importance of a positive orientation toward innovation and change.

Within this setting, education was widely perceived as a central means for social mobility and the attainment of a more modern and comfortable lifestyle, going beyond the often rural lifestyles typical of the prewar period. That is, within the rapidly changing social and economic structure, education was considered not just as a means of getting a job, but also as a way of moving beyond one's parents' station. This ambition was, notably, not limited to the urban middle class. Many women who obtained senior high school degrees in the 1960s derived from rural backgrounds, and these women describe their own journey from high school to an urban office job as a common aspiration.

Miura Natsu's experience was characteristic in this respect. Miura grew up in a large family of farmers. While her older siblings did not complete senior high school, instead taking on farming like their parents, Miura, who was among the youngest of her siblings, was able to complete senior high school, not only because family finances had improved but also because, as she saw it, senior high school attendance had by then become a common pattern for her generation. As she relates: "When I was young, it was important to try to finish senior high school; that would mean that you would be able to get the kind of job you wanted. My older siblings quit school after middle school, mostly for economic reasons. But when I was that age, it had become more normal to go to senior high school." With the decline of farming even girls were expected to obtain an education that would help them land a more secure position in the modern sector. Together with other girls from her high school, Miura was recruited via her school for a job in Tokyo, from which she launched her independent life outside of the confines of rural family life. These new educational and employment opportunities, notably, also had clear gender dimensions. Miura was aware of the difficult life facing women as wives, workers, and mothers in her hometown and was eager to get away and to free herself from these constraints.

Nakada Ikuko, who had seen her own mother suffer from a difficult relationship with her in-laws and engage in low-paid work, was motivated by her mother's advice to pursue education and better employment also for her own sake. She describes her situation as follows:

> My mother said I should go to senior high school; otherwise, I would only be able to get manual jobs, which was something she herself had experienced. My mother did piecework at home (*naishoku*) when the children were small, and then worked in various jobs outside while the children were in day care, mostly for financial reasons. My father worked as a driver...but there were ups and downs in the business, so it did not bring in much [money].

Nakada took for granted that she would be working as a woman and a mother, as her salary, even if low, would be needed to contribute to the family income. Her ambitions about pursuing higher educational attainment and employment opportunities in the modern sector also highlighted her awareness of her mother's hardships in working primarily in low-skilled manual jobs while raising a family. Nakada felt motivated to obtain a senior high school degree not only to be able to move beyond manual labor, but also to secure herself and her family a lifestyle with greater comfort and stability.

University graduates of this generation, who constituted a small and rather privileged minority among my interviewees, were similarly ambitious to pursue new opportunities in education and to move beyond their parents' lifestyles. Yet, unlike high school graduates, who often spoke about the material hardships of their family life, university graduates' stories were more often marked by the entrepreneurial spirit of fathers who had successfully engaged in business in the early postwar period. Hara Tomoko, for instance, grew up in a Japanese family that had moved to Manchuria during World War II, where they owned a large estate and led an affluent life during the war. Returning to Japan after the end of the war, they had lost not only their estate in Manchuria but also their land and assets in Japan due to land reform. Unable to return to farming, they instead successfully built up a printing business. Engaging successfully in a business that made use of modern technology translated not only into a good income but also into social status within their local community. Hara explains: "Because [my father] was dealing with new things, such as printing, in a small business in the local area, and since he employed some people for his business, I was seen as the daughter of the 'boss.'" Although her parents had not attended university themselves, the affluence and status afforded by their business allowed them to take for granted that their children would enroll at a university and would similarly take advantage of the opportunities of their times.

This successful pursuit of innovation and independent business on the part of parents also came with an emphasis on personal independence and on confidence in education as a means to foster the future opportunities and independence of their children. Watanabe Takako, for instance, grew up in the countryside in a family that owned a factory. Her parents saw education as an essential means to ensuring their children's success in life. She describes their motivation for sending her to university: "My parents had the idea that you should be able to support yourself; even if other things are lost, [an education] cannot be taken away. So all three [of us siblings] went to study in Tokyo." In light of their own wartime and postwar experiences of loss and rebuilding, Watanabe's parents considered education not just as a reflection of social status, but also as a personal asset and a source of economic and personal independence in war and peace.

This view of education as a means of social mobility was particularly central in the case of fathers who, unlike those of Hara and Watanabe, did not already come from relatively well-to-do backgrounds and had to work very hard to establish themselves against the odds in the postwar era. Nakamura Fusako's father was such a person. Nakamura's father had served as a soldier during World War II and was the only one to have survived from his division, an experience that marked his life and outlook in the long term. Returning to Japan, he built a business by making use of quite ruthless tactics. According to Nakamura, "My father would make more of his products than needed and would make his clients buy them. Even though he had no education, and even though he did not go to university, he had a lot of knowledge and ideas. He had a lot of power and influence." Having survived the war, and needing to restart his life without any assets or education, Nakamura's father was acutely aware of the disadvantages he faced vis-à-vis others who had a university education. He would have to rely on his own survival strategies to succeed in life. As a consequence, he had a clear understanding of the benefits of an education and sent his daughter, who herself was not particularly ambitious, to study at university.

This appreciation of education was also evident in families whose businesses were less successful. Ueda Atsuko's father was himself raised in a farmer's family with very limited means, and although he was able to establish his own family business, everyday life remained hard. Ueda grew up conscious of the barriers and limitations posed by a low level of educational attainment and limited assets. As she recalls:

> My father had a lot of siblings and they were farmers. He was not the eldest but the second, so he was kind of in between.... And they were poor.... Neither [of my parents] had much of an education.... My mother would have liked to be able to write better, and in the case of my father, his youngest brother apparently went to university, so he probably also wanted to go to university [but couldn't]. It's a symbol of the people from this generation; those who were born in the late 1920s and early 1930s, so many became rich. So he was extremely frugal and hardworking.

Precisely because of the upward mobility of many members of this generation, the inability to be successful sharpened the sense of disadvantage and the appreciation of the opportunities afforded by having an education. Fathers' own struggles, without much else but their own hard work and effort to build their future amidst a rapidly growing and increasingly affluent society, clearly strengthened their appreciation of the value of education and of the opportunities it offered as well as of the long-term disadvantages a lack of educational attainment could produce.

Ueda's account of her family life, however, also raises other important issues: the role and position of mothers in the family and fathers' visions of their daughters' future. That is, although fathers were eager to embrace the new opportunities and to move beyond prewar social structures, they also derived from a generation where a patriarchal family life and gendered life courses were taken for granted. Suda Yoko, who grew up in a rural community and within a farm household, describes the gender paradigms of her childhood as follows:

> It was a very patriarchal kind of village. The relationship between the bride and her mother-in-law was always difficult. It was a very closed and unsociable place. Also, my parents were very patriarchal in attitude. My father decided everything, and as for the daughter, [I was told] "A girl's happiness is to get married and help out with the family business." Until I left home, I also thought, "Because I am a woman, I just have to live with it."

Relationships within the family could also be guided by this principle. Nakamura Fusako acutely felt the subservient role of her mother:

> At home, life was military-style. Absolute obedience, that is [what my father's military background] brought into the family.... My mother was a woman with a traditional lifestyle; she did what my father said. She was that type of person. My father held women in disdain (*josei besshi*). He thought my mother should follow him. It was that kind of family.

While fathers were eager to move beyond old social structures in their work life, therefore, a rigid gender hierarchy within the family was not necessarily open to question.

Yet, fathers who had ambitions for themselves and were open to innovation and change, while keeping their families under a patriarchal order, did evoke questioning of their views. Even if women did not find a vocabulary to articulate resistance, a number of them expressed a deep sense of discomfort with their mother's situation. Nakamura, who otherwise spoke with much modesty and calm, emotionally noted, "I never wanted to live like my mother!" Aware of her own father's struggles to make it in business without any assets or education, Nakamura felt the same sense of disadvantage and confinement in her father's treatment of her mother. Other women also highlighted objections against their mothers' dependence on their fathers. As Hara Tomoko puts it: "In the old days, a husband could have affairs and do whatever, and my mother, even if my father had an affair and a lover, and there were rumors all around, she would have stayed with him until her death. But when I saw how my mother lived, I thought I would never tolerate that."

Daughters acutely felt the inherently unequal marital relationship of their parents, and also their mothers' lack of resources to challenge their situation. The latter was attributed by some women to their mothers' lack of education. As Ueda Atsuko, whose mother appeared to be barely literate, observes, "I always felt pity for her, being scolded by my father for lacking 'culture' and sophistication. She was not even good at cooking." From Ueda's perspective, her mother's subordination was a consequence not only of patriarchal ideology, but also of her acute lack of educational and cultural capital. From these women's perspectives, therefore, social mobility was not just a question of employment and income; it was also a matter of improving their own position as women within the family.

When it came time to decide about a daughter's higher education, the clash between a father's ambitions for upward mobility, on the one hand, and a gendered view of the children's future, on the other, moved even more to the foreground. To be sure, some fathers simply sent all their children to university in the city, in light of the lack of opportunities back in the countryside. In other cases, however, the need and value of a daughter's education was drawn into question. This was by no means unusual. As Brinton (1993) has shown, until the 1980s girls' education had significantly less priority in many households than that of boys. Ueda Atsuko's experience illustrates this situation:

> [My father] really wanted my eldest brother to go [to university]. But he said girls don't need an education. When I said I wanted to go to junior college, and wanted to go to a private high school in Tokyo, he was against it at the

beginning. When I continued to say I wanted to go, he said that since you are going to invest all that money, try and do something useful. So I enrolled in the business division in high school and after that I wanted to go to junior college. He endlessly complained that women really don't need an education. It made me wonder, "Really, women don't need an education?"

Fuelled by her mother's unhappiness and subordination, which she partly attributed to the lack of education, as well as by her father's struggle to do well in business, Ueda found her father's lack of support for her own education unacceptable.

Not all parents were resistant to their daughters' attendance of university, but the purpose of a woman's higher education remained a novel and uncertain topic. Kamata Toshiko, who herself indicated to her parents that she wanted to continue on to university, as she enjoyed studying, relates: "My parents did not quite understand why their daughter, why I wanted to study. But when I said I wanted to go [to university], they did support me. But they could not give me advice on what to do." Although her parents had achieved a comparatively high level of education in the prewar period, they were at a loss as to what to advise a girl to study at university. "When I had to choose my second foreign language, once I was admitted [to university], I had to choose between German, French, and Chinese. I asked them about what to do, and she [my mother] said, 'Well, you are a girl, so….' I wondered: 'Why does it matter that I am a girl? What does it have to do with foreign languages?'"

Although she was given the opportunity to attend university without questioning, Kamata remained well aware that her parents had different expectations regarding her and her brother's future: "My parents gave all kinds of advice to my brother, regarding where to look for a job, but they didn't tell me a thing." While given the opportunity to attend university, therefore, she pursued her university degree with little guidance or advice from her parents and with no clear idea as to what exactly a university education could or should entail. Although women did obtain educational credentials, therefore, they often did so without a clear sense of the meaning and purpose of those credentials.

Within the changing social and economic environment of the 1960s, therefore, the attainment of a senior high school or university degree constituted a qualification that promised real opportunities. Raised by a generation marked by the losses of war and the promises of the rapidly expanding postwar economy, many women felt encouraged to pursue the educational opportunities of their times under the promise of greater affluence and a more comfortable family life. But social mobility, from the perspective of these young women, was not just about improving one's material conditions. Just as their fathers were eager to embrace innovation and new opportunities to achieve a higher social status, so were daughters inspired to seek out education and employment as a means to move beyond the patriarchal family structures of their upbringing.

GENDER AND EMPLOYMENT BEFORE THE EEOL

The ambition to pursue a future beyond the confines of the patriarchal family of their upbringing was also noticeable in women's accounts of their search for employment. While employment itself was not unusual for women whose mothers had mostly worked in farming or the family business, the possibility of employment in factories or offices in the city offered a unique outlook on a modern, and more independent, lifestyle. For senior high school graduates, in particular, the period of the 1960s and early 1970s appeared to be rich in opportunities for employment. Some women from rural senior high schools were able to find employment in the form of group recruitment (*shûdan shûshoku*) facilitated by their senior high school. Sato Mina followed this route. Her parents were farmers, but because there were no work opportunities in the countryside, she joined a group of other female graduates who were recommended by their school for work in a factory, which included residence in a dormitory. Others looked independently for employment. Nakada Ikuko, for instance, directly applied for an office job after graduating from senior high school, eventually working herself into a secure position as an accounting clerk. As university enrollment still remained fairly uncommon, the completion of a senior high school degree came with ample employment opportunities in the rapidly expanding economy of the 1960s and early 1970s, propelling female senior high school graduates to pursue an independent life beyond their parental household.

The urge to escape rural life in some cases featured strongly in women's stories of coming of age. Sato Mina notes:

> Because I came from the countryside, I have seen a poor way of living and life before women had the right to free speech. I saw these sorts of things, and I heard the gossip of the mothers-in-law, the husbands, and so on when my siblings came together. I came to understand that marriage is not always easy. I thought it would be quite hard.... I wanted to live far away from my parents and to work. I felt very strongly about that.

Sato's drive for personal independence was not consciously informed by readings in feminism, yet she intuitively felt an urge to free herself from the confinement she associated with living in an extended family in the countryside. Sato hoped to find independence in the city, and pursue a life that would not be dominated by the gender hierarchy that was predominant in the family of her upbringing.

University graduates, likewise, shared this urge to find a place in the city but, unlike high school graduates, faced a more complex situation in the world of work. On the one hand, having come predominantly from families running a small business in rural areas, like high school graduates few university graduates considered returning to their families. Some were even explicitly told to stay away. Hara Tomoko's parents told her: "There is no work here in the countryside, so don't you come back. We have our hands full by ourselves." Others felt the urge to remain financially independent, so as not to worry their parents. As Watanabe Takako says, "I wanted an income that would enable me to make ends meet somehow.... If you are out of school, but can not live from your own salary, your parents would worry." Their petty bourgeois background not only inspired them to seek out new opportunities, but also furnished their urge to become, and remain, independent from their parents.

On the other hand, getting a job as a female university graduate in the early 1970s was difficult. If anything, finding a job was harder with a university education than with a high school degree (Brinton 1993; Hara and Seiyama 2005 [1999]). The challenges of finding employment and making ends meet on their own were clearly present in the stories of searching for job opportunities. Nakamura Fusako remembers: "Those days, on the contrary, there were [no jobs] for university graduates." The lack of work opportunities had in their view partly to do with gendered job advertisements. Kamata Toshiko notes: "When I graduated from university in 1971, it was rare to find a job advertisement that would ask for a 'woman' and not a 'man.' Most [women's] jobs were for teachers, so I tried to get the teacher's qualification." Searching for employment before the introduction of the Equal Employment Opportunity Law therefore came with very few options to which to apply themselves. Hara Tomoko describes her experience:

> When I was about to graduate, I started to think about what to do. If you wonder why I decided to get a teaching license, you know, those days, for a woman to get herself a job in the future.... Most young ladies studying in Tokyo those days were not planning to find employment. The trend those days was that except for those who had the goal of getting a specific job based on qualifications such as day care provider, kindergarten teacher, school teacher, or nurse, others would just get a regular job, and the women and the companies thought they would work for one to two years, perhaps two to three years [and then get married].

While there were some clerical office jobs, in the form of short-term secretarial work, available to women (cf. Rohlen 1974), unless a woman entered a specific feminized profession, long-term employment for university graduates appeared unlikely. Distinctive about this particular generation of women university graduates, therefore, is not only that they obtained a university education at a time when this was still very unusual; they were also unique in their drive to find employment at a time when companies offered few if any long-term employment prospects to female university graduates.

In this setting, kindergarten and school teaching seemed particularly attractive, as these offered a unique opportunity for long-term employment. Yet, few actually succeeded in maintaining a teaching job. Nakamura Fusako, who took a teaching license at a professional school "because tuition was cheap, and the exam was not difficult," worked as a teacher for two years, but she damaged her health and quit. Kamata Toshiko also quit after a year as a kindergarten teacher.

> I thought I should try it. But in the end, I got tired of the energy of the children. All of a sudden, I was the head teacher for thirty children. I had children who only came to kindergarten the year before entering school. So they were not used to kindergarten at the time. Only the children from my class would run around, and would not form a line in an orderly fashion at the sports events. In the end, it became really hard. I thought I would not like to become one of those strict teachers, so in the end I just quit.

Hara Tomoko similarly notes: "I got myself a teaching license, but when it came to teaching in practice, I realized quickly that I was not really made for it." While being a female university graduate qualified them for the profession, it did not guarantee a good match with their personality or abilities.

Office jobs by contrast, were easier to get into but tended not to come with the possibility of long-term employment or, for that matter, the opportunity for advancement. Hara Tomoko explains:

> I found a job through the mediation of my school. I was told already at the job interview that women were expected to work for no more than two or three years. [My job] did not require me to be good at writing; it was mainly about producing materials for a monthly conference at a time when there were no computers or copy machines. Apart from that, it was enough to "pour tasty tea."

The working world, in other words, offered few rewards or challenges to women university and college graduates, which left some believing that long-term employment for women was simply not an option. Ueda Atsuko adds:

> I job-hopped quite a bit, doing accounting. There wasn't really a job that I really wanted to do.... I did not work in the same job for a long time. There was no image of a woman working for a long time; there were no career-track jobs for women at the time.... It was always the same every day, always the same work, the same employees, and others married and quit.... I actually liked [my job] at the first company; it was a good company. But because all

the others left, I felt I had been there for a long time. That's right, at the time, there were no female division chiefs (*buchô*), so there was no role model. I didn't even think of it, so I always did work assisting others. So after a few years others quit, so I thought of quitting as well.

Having been raised by a family in independent business, Ueda had no clear sense of what a career as a white-collar employee should look like. Aware of the drudgery and repetition of feminized office jobs, she saw no future for herself in the world of work and, instead, followed the convention of quitting her jobs before she could get too bored.

Where women high school graduates seemed to accept and cherish the work opportunities they could find, their counterparts among university graduates faced a working world that offered few opportunities and rewards, as employment among women university graduates was still relatively uncommon and equal employment opportunities not assured by law. As educational pioneers, they had courageously pursued the opportunities offered to them, but after graduation seemed to face a dead-end street with few guarantees for long-term employment or economic self-reliance.

MARRIAGE AND ECONOMIC INDEPENDENCE

In light of the pioneering educational and work experiences of the women of this generation, one may expect that they also entered the topic of marriage with alternative perspectives. Raised by families where patriarchal family relations associated with the *ie* family system remained common, many indeed seemed critical of prewar norms of family relations. That is, they associated marriage and family with the often unequal power relationship of their parents, rather than with the growing pressures facing housewives and education mothers during the heyday of the salaryman family. As a consequence, their concerns about marriage focused more on their relationship to their partner in marriage and their personal independence, than on the role and pressures facing women as housewives and mothers.

Significant about their stories of getting married is that many enjoyed considerable freedom in their choice of their partner in marriage. Kimura Yu, who had to become economically independent when leaving middle school because her parents passed away when she was young, for instance, had no influence from parents to consider when thinking about marriage. Following the convention of marriage mediation at the time, her colleagues at work took over the role of connecting her with a partner. She matter-of-factly recounts: "When I was 29, a co-worker introduced me to my future husband." Although she decided independently about her marriage, she remarks that "[i]t was not a love marriage." Marriage, in this case, seemed an inevitable life stage and means to form a family, in sum, a practical matter.

Nakada Ikuko also seemed more concerned with material aspects than personal affection in her considerations about her partner in marriage. Having lost her mother at an early age and having struggled with the unstable economic and social environment of her upbringing as a teenager, Nakada carefully considered her future husband's trustworthiness as a breadwinner and his financial viability. "He had grown up with a single mother and always paid his mother money [for his upkeep], so I thought that was a good sign." Nakada seemed to take for granted that she would get married and form a family, yet was also keen to achieve a certain sense of economic stability by choosing a partner she considered as a reliable breadwinner.

There were however also women who were concerned about maintaining their personal independence, and seemed more cautious about getting married. Miura Natsu, whom we saw earlier voice her trepidations about marriage, explains:

> I married late.... I did not really want to get married. I thought I would like to work and not marry, and even if I married, I wanted to find a workplace where I could work nevertheless. But I didn't find such place. And because I had reached a certain age, people started bothering me, saying, "You should get married." I changed my mind after being told by other people as well, and I got to know someone at the same company who I thought I would not mind marrying. And so I married, at quite a high age.... It's not that I had a specific vision of life [and therefore was skeptical about marriage].... I thought maybe I could try it out just once.... I made him promise that I could continue to work after marriage.

Miura did not articulate a particular ideological stance about marriage, yet, as we saw earlier, showed a keen awareness of the subordination and hardship her married cousins in the countryside experienced. As she saw employment as the singular means for maintaining a certain level of personal independence in marriage, but combining employment and marriage was at best difficult at the time, this also meant that Miura entered marriage with a great level of unease.

Indeed, combining work and motherhood in the city was a complex affair. Kimura Yu, who due to a low family income moved into public housing with her husband and child, was forced to quit working temporarily after giving birth because of a lack of funds and facilities for day care. As public housing caters to families with a very low income, she, however, became active together with other working mothers resident in the same residential building in organizing an informal day care facility. "It was necessary financially for mothers to work," she observes. At first, they shared the bill in paying a mother living in the same apartment complex to take care of their children. Later on, they lobbied for and helped establish a private day care facility. Her story is not unusual in that she raised her children at a time when the acute lack of day care facilities and the hardships facing working mothers became more of a public issue (Fuse 1984). For high school graduates who raised children in the 1970s, the slogan "as many day care centers as postal mailboxes" evoked much nostalgic memory.

Employment in the city, as opposed to the countryside, therefore, also challenged mothers to find the means to accommodate work and family in new ways. Whereas their mothers had worked on the family farm surrounded by relatives, high school graduates working in factories and office jobs in the city faced considerable challenges in balancing work and parenthood without the support of family members. This, however, also meant that some women more consciously negotiated the shape that their modern marriage would take. Yonekawa Sachiko, a high school graduate who pursued a career in the entertainment industry as an independent entrepreneur, for instance, negotiated the division of labor in the home with her partner. One of the first arguments they had, she recalls, was about housework. She demanded a 50:50 share while he demanded 70:30; they later settled for 60:40. "I guess that's why I am not suitable for marriage," she sighs.

The fact that particularly female high school graduates' incomes were often contributing to the household income, however, also offered possibilities for alternative arrangements. When Kimura's spouse quit his job over an argument with his superior and decided to become a writer, she had no objections to becoming the main breadwinner of the family even if this meant constrained finances. The newly gained economic opportunities and independence from the family of origin, therefore, did generate a space for alternative marital and family relations. While these women fell short of realizing their ambitions—as they separated while their children were small—their stories highlight not only the impact of educational and employment opportunities, but also the ambitions and visions of social mobility and gender equality that informed their approach to employment, family, and marriage.

As compared to high school graduates, some university graduates were considerably more explicit in their critique and outspoken in their resistance to marriage. Nakamura Fusako explains: "With regards to marriage, I did not have a positive outlook on marriage. I was not convinced. I could not go forward [and get married]." Having observed the troubles of their parents' relationship, some had difficulties finding a positive meaning in marriage. Hara Tomoko adds: "Because I started out with a bad notion of family, I started out with a negative image. I could only think of things to disapprove of…. I just thought, I don't want to become like that…. I didn't want to become like my mother." Having grown up largely with parents who had entered an arranged marriage, the conflicts and lack of affection between their parents and the dependence of their mothers on their fathers made these women feel cautious about what to expect in marriage.

A number of women also simply did not envision marriage and family as a necessary part of their personal life course. As Kamata Toshiko, for example, remarked, "I was a typical single working woman at the time. I never thought I would become a mother." Finding employment and making ends meet was clearly a challenge even for university graduates of this generation, yet many seemed driven to avoid the dependence and subordination experienced by their mothers. Takenaka Hiroko was most explicit about her views of marriage:

> A lot of people still think along the lines of the *ie* family system. That the eldest son will become the next head of the family. I personally have no aspiration for becoming dependent on a husband, and I don't really understand those who think it is evident that they should be dependent and only work part-time [to stay below the level of income to be treated as their husband's dependant for tax purposes].... There are some women who want to marry or have a boyfriend. But not me. On the contrary, I can't be bothered. There are different views on the necessity of having a husband.

Takenaka, notably, was among the few with a firm economic base, as she had taken over her parents' family business and owned property already in her twenties, which also made it possible for her to afford such views.

Not all were quite as resistant to marriage, however. In light of the fact that most had considerable liberties when it came to the choice of a partner, they also had a greater role in shaping their marriage. Living at a distance from their parents, many women formed relationships freely and largely without the knowledge or mediation of their family, as they lived independently in the city. Watanabe Takako explained: "My parents were the kind of people who would say: 'You decide yourself and you do it yourself, that's all.'" Hara Tomoko, moreover, lived together with her future husband before getting married. "[My parents] were not the kind of people who would resist if I was going to tell them I was planning to get married. Because they were busy with their own life. It's not that they didn't care, but they would just sort of say: 'Ah, really, [you are getting married?] Great!'" Parents' appreciation of and support for the idea of personal independence also granted women a considerable freedom in the choice of their partners and lifestyles.

In practice, motherhood and marriage in many cases "happened" without much ceremony and, more concretely, as a consequence of an unplanned pregnancy. Several women who had no plans to get married faced an unexpected pregnancy in their late twenties or early thirties. Watanabe Takako, for instance, explains: "I am not the type who loves children. For me the prospect of having a child was scary. I did not come to like it, and I was scared of giving birth to something just like myself. I was quite resistant. But in the end, well, it was a shotgun marriage (*dekichatta kekkon*)." As a consequence, a number of women rushed into marriage even if they did not expect the relationship to last. As Hara Tomoko recalls, "I ended up leaving a lot of things aside. For the future of the child, we should try to get along, do the papers…do things properly. That's what I felt strongly." Marriage, in such cases, constituted a framework to legitimize birth, rather than being the focus of an intimate conjugal relationship.

Takenaka Hiroko's case further underlines this point. Takenaka found herself unexpectedly pregnant, and initially had no intention to marry. Facing pressure from her family, however, she succumbed:

> I thought things should be fine [without getting married] but my family found that difficult to accept. Therefore, my brother talked to my partner and it was decided that at least we should do the [marriage] papers—really just the papers—we actually never lived together…. One of the benefits is that my family name changed [indicating marriage], and also for the child, you know, Japanese society treats children born outside of marriage rather harshly.

Fearful of the stigma facing their child, a number of women entered unstable relationships or paper marriages to protect their unborn children.

Age was another consideration. While few saw becoming a mother as a primary goal in life, unlike marriage, motherhood attracted fewer doubts and it was the urge to become a mother, rather than to have a partner, that seemed to feature strongly in some women's decisions to get married when finding themselves pregnant. Hara Tomoko continues:

> I discussed [my relationship and unplanned pregnancy] with my parents and others, and some said I should separate if this is what things were like. But because I was twenty-seven or twenty-eight, I thought at the time that I should have a child before turning thirty. I also worried that if I had an abortion, I might not be able to have a child for the rest of my life.

The ability to become a mother, in this case, took precedence over considerations about the actual partner in marriage.

In addition, the frustrations they faced in the world of work made some think of marriage as a better option. Ueda Atsuko explains:

> Well, after all, I really wanted children. So if you want to have children, the age you can still marry is the age you can still have children. Now, some people have children later, at an older age, but at the time you thought it should be in one's twenties and I wondered, "Will I just go on without giving birth?" I didn't have a lot of fun working; otherwise, things might have been different. But, by coincidence, there was someone who asked me to marry, and I thought maybe this is the last chance. If I don't take this chance, I may not have a second chance. Well, I made a mistake in getting married. It would have been different if I had a job I enjoyed.

Ueda had been ambitious in trying out various avenues in education and employment but, bored and frustrated in a dead-end job as an Office Lady, she became more invested in getting married when she reached her late twenties.

Having grown up in a period of rapid economic development and change, both high school and university graduate women from the pre-Bubble generation enjoyed many new opportunities. But they also faced the challenge of forging new and unprecedented lifestyles in a rapidly evolving economy and society. They represent a pioneering generation of women, eager to leave the hard material circumstances and patriarchal structures of their childhood behind and to pursue equality and independence in employment and marriage, inspired by the promise of meritocratic principles of the postwar period and by the spirit of social mobility that had informed their childhoods. What defined their approach toward their own life course and future was not simply their fathers' social status, but rather more so their attitudes and dispositions toward education and new employment opportunities.

Education, in this case, was not merely considered a marker of social class, but also a means and mechanism that would facilitate upward mobility and economic independence. This pursuit of social mobility, however, also had important gender dimensions. Driven by the pioneering spirit of their generation, and during a period marked by expanding employment opportunities, many embraced the idea of equal opportunities to achieve greater personal and economic independence but came to apply this idea also to their understanding of marriage. While not necessarily resistant to marriage and motherhood per se, these women embraced their future in a way that did not rest solely on exploring new opportunities in education and employment, but also meant looking for new models and possibilities in marital relations. Notably, rather than being focused on the postwar ideal and role of the housewife, their resistance focused largely on the unequal and patriarchal relationships of the families of their upbringing. What defines the pre-Bubble generation's life course and dispositions, therefore, is not simply a rejection of marriage and family in place of economic independence. Instead, their stories highlight the gendered aspects of social mobility and the pursuit of a more egalitarian marital relationship as part of the promise and spirit of opportunity of the early postwar period.

Chapter Three

The Bubble Generation

Kondo Naoko grew up in a residential district in Tokyo in the 1970s in the heyday of the Bubble economy. Her childhood seemed both idyllic and unremarkable, possessing many of the characteristic features attributed to the typical salaryman family lifestyle of this period. Her father had a stable job as an employee, and her mother stayed home to take care of the children, like most mothers in the neighborhood did. She avoided the stressful period of "exam hell" by taking exams early, entering her desired school from middle school rather than high school. Interested in art, she then enrolled in an art academy.

As she approached graduation, however, the order and predictability that had thus far defined her life began to wane. While many of her friends had already settled into a job, she felt aimless in her search. In a last-minute move, she found employment with a publishing company. Yet, although she felt fulfilled by her job, she grew increasingly concerned and restless about getting married as she approached age thirty. In anticipation of marriage, she quit her job and traveled abroad for some time. She then married an acquaintance shortly after her return. Within less than a year, however, the marriage fell apart. She divorced and moved out a few months after giving birth to her daughter.

Troubled by the sudden turn of events, she reflects, "My family was a normal family—among relatives and family, nobody was divorced." Kondo had been raised in a conventional middle-class family and experienced a seemingly unremarkable and conventional lifestyle until then; becoming a single mother was, needless to say, not an anticipated lifestyle. Yet, her experience was not unique, and reflects the ambivalence and contradiction that has come to define women's approaches to marriage, motherhood, and employment in the 1990s.

One of the most distinctive differences between the pre-Bubble generation, born in the 1950s, and the Bubble generation, born between 1960 and the early 1970s, is the rising prominence of the idealized salaryman family and full-time housewife as the central discursive context within which marriage and motherhood was discussed. Whereas the pre-Bubble generation reminisced about the family life of their childhood as a relic from the past, the Bubble generation grew up in the heyday of the professional housewife (Honda 2000), where the ideal of the salaryman family was widely considered omnipresent and the status quo.

Also the latter generation's disposition toward their life course differed. The family lives of the pre-Bubble generation were, as we have seen, marked by innovation, change, and a focus on social mobility; the life courses of the Bubble generation, by contrast, were characterized by a sense of stability and predictability (cf. Brinton 1993; Kelly 1993), and a preoccupation with the maintenance of a middle-class status and lifestyle. A gender division of labor in the home and the role of the housewife and education mother came to be taken for granted, and a university education was seen as a normal extension of youth rather than as a goal or achievement in life. Whereas women from the pre-Bubble generation had largely grown up outside of the city with self-employed parents, the Bubble generation, who came of age in the late 1970s and 1980s, more often grew up in families of salaried employees, with mothers who stayed at home to take care of the household and children, in short, the typical middle-class salaryman family. As a consequence, marriage, motherhood, and family took on new meanings. Under the influence of the postwar Japanese family system, marriage and motherhood were no longer simply life stages and gender roles; they now came to constitute important milestones in women's life courses and central symbols of their social status and identity.

In this chapter, I examine the lived realities of the postwar Japanese family system through the lens of the life stories of single mothers from the Bubble generation. In contrast with the childhoods of the previous generation of single mothers, their stories highlight the normative presence of the salaryman and professional housewife ideal and the impact of this ideal on their personal outlook on marriage, motherhood, and employment. Whereas single mothers from the previous generation were often pioneers, forging new pathways in education, employment, marriage, and women's independence, the stories of the Bubble generation are characterized by conformity, and highlight the growing pressures associated with marriage and motherhood not only as a life stage but also as a source of status and a symbol of personal achievement. Their reflections on divorce and single motherhood, moreover, highlight the growing contradictions and frictions of the salaryman family ideal, and the difficulties of pursuing the anticipated life course of a married wife and mother.

A "NORMAL" FAMILY LIFE

One of the key characteristics of the stories of childhood recalled by women from the Bubble generation was that their narratives of childhood and family life, as well as their ambitions for their future, were often framed by the ideal of the middle-class salaryman family. Their stories not only confirmed the perceived markers of a normative middle-class family lifestyle, but also highlighted its appeal and role in affirming their own status and identity as members of the mainstream middle class of the Bubble economy.

A key concept in the narratives from this generation was the "normalcy" of their upbringing. When asked about their childhood and family background, many hastened to emphasize the fact that they came from a "normal" middle-class family. Tanaka Miyuki, for instance, grew up in a well-to-do family in Tokyo. Her father was a professional with his own practice, while her mother stayed at home to take care of the couple's two children. "It's really normal, isn't it?" she remarks a few minutes into our interview. She entered private school from an early age, which more or less guaranteed entrance into a prestigious private university upon graduation. She was interested in her studies, but also eager to marry and, with her parents' encouragement, she married a successful businessman and became a housewife at the age of twenty-five.

Tanaka was unique in actually living the "Japanese Dream," pursuing a picture-book life course from elite schooling to a comfortable life as a full-time housewife. As White (2002) has argued, actual family lifestyles were considerably more diverse in practice. Even if women considered themselves to have grown up in a "normal" salaryman family, there was variation in their living conditions and material welfare. Kumagai Akemi, a university graduate whose father worked as a salaryman, described her upbringing as follows: "I grew up in a typical three-generation family, with my grandparents and one elder sister. It was a very normal life (*heihei bonbon*), a poor life. My father was a normal salaryman, and until I entered university we had a quite normal life." The "normal" life of a salaryman family, for Kumagai, did not necessarily entail a sense of affluence, even if she felt that her family led a typical middle-class lifestyle.

Also in the case of Tokunaga Asami, whose father worked in a white-collar job, material affluence was not central to her concept of middle class. She recounts: "Our living standard was probably not bad given the time period, but because we lived in company housing and often moved, we actually had a lot of loans. A typical nuclear family." But after the birth of another child, the family's finances went downhill. "From when I was quite small, I was told: 'There is no money.'" While Tokunaga felt her family belonged to the middle class, this self-perception was not necessarily supported by her family's material circumstances. The defining element of the feeling of belonging to the middle class was not so much economic affluence, but rather the modern lifestyle associated with families headed by a white-collar salaryman.

For women themselves, the completion of a university degree was another central marker of their middle-classness. Unlike the university graduates from the pre-Bubble generation, those from the Bubble generation mostly took for granted the ability to go to university as an extension of their youth rather than as a goal or achievement in life. That women would also enroll in university was by then no longer a point of discussion. Kumagai Akemi explains her motivation to enroll at university: "It's a little embarrassing to say, but in a way probably very Japanese. I had no particular goals in going to university. My elder sister went, so I also went to university." Where university graduates born in the 1950s were clearly aware of the exceptional educational opportunities they enjoyed and the challenges of exploring this uncharted territory, women growing up during the Bubble period experienced university education as a mass phenomenon and little more than a life stage in their predictable middle-class life course.

Access to a university education appeared to be so much taken for granted among university graduates that few articulated particular ambitions in education and employment, despite the encouragement of their parents. Imamura Naoko, for instance, grew up with parents who both had professional qualifications and were working full-time. Yet, her parents' commitment to their children's education clearly outshone the children's personal ambitions. She explains:

> My parents were quite strongly devoted to education. They made me study a lot from when I was in elementary school. I also went to a good private middle school and high school. From there I went straight to university. I liked food, so I went into the biology department.... Because both of my parents worked, I did not feel any resistance to the idea of working as a woman. Because I am the oldest daughter, there were high expectations of me from my parents. They really supported me in my studies. But when I was at university, I did not study. I went to a sports club and kept busy with that all the time.

The drive to take advantage of educational opportunities clearly had tapered off within the changing environment of the Bubble economy. Where the women of the previous generation often had to push for their right to obtain a higher education, the women of the Bubble generation more often appeared ambivalent, and lacked the same ambition to take advantage of educational opportunities and take ownership of their life course and personal future.

Yet, while it seemed obvious for Kumagai and Imamura that they would complete a university degree in any case, access to a university education could not be taken for granted by everyone. With jobs in abundance and a senior high school education becoming almost universal, the period of the

Bubble economy might be expected to be a time when class differences were much less visible than in other periods. Yet, high school graduates from low-income families displayed a clear awareness of differences in their opportunities and in their ability to live up to the normative middle-class family ideal. To be sure, fathers of high school graduates were also often employees, some with a stable "salaryman" job and others working as skilled or semi-skilled manual workers. Mothers, too, in a number of cases stayed at home. Yet, there were qualitative differences in living conditions, as well as in outlook on education and employment.

Whereas a typical salaryman and his family were expected to own their home in the suburbs, families with a comparatively low income more often lived in smaller apartments in the city or in public housing units. Sakai Yoshimi, who described herself as coming from a low-income family, seemed very aware of disparities in living conditions when she was a child. When I asked her to tell me about her family background at the very beginning of the interview, she stated: "My mother was a professional housewife and my father a company employee. I was the second child. But I grew up in a household with a comparatively low income." Probed about what living with a "comparatively low income" meant, she explained:

> We lived in an apartment all along. It was an old apartment, without a bath. This is where I grew up. When I was a child, this was still common, such households. Middle-class households, they lived in a house with a private bath, but about a third of our class lived in private apartments without baths, when I was in elementary school. We all went to the public bath (*sentô*) and there I would meet with classmates, and say "Hey, what's up?" That's how we lived.

Sakai had no misgivings about her upbringing. If anything, the communal bath evoked nostalgic memories and a sense of community. Yet, she was keenly aware that living in a small apartment without a bath was a clear marker of lower-class status. From her perspective, it was not just her father's occupation as an employee but, more importantly, differences in living conditions that defined her lower-class family origins.

Even more central to the stories of women who grew up in low-income families, however, was the impact of their families' finances on their educational opportunities. While most university graduates barely mentioned the name of their high school and saw a university education as a self-evident part of their educational trajectory, senior high school graduates were more often aware of the limits of their educational opportunities. Kato Minako, for example, grew up in a working-class family; her father, who had only completed middle school, worked in a skilled manual job with a stable contract, while her mother stayed at home while the children were small. Her story of her youth expressed a sense of stability and described a settled lifestyle. "I went to a local elementary and middle school in [the district where we lived].... Once I completed middle school, I went to high school. I went to [the local] municipal high school, nearby here." Unlike university graduates, who barely mentioned their high school years, Kato proudly presented her enrollment in a specific senior high school as a major milestone and personal achievement.

But where Kato Minako's story expressed a sense of normalcy and confidence about her education, the stories of high school graduates from backgrounds with even tighter finances place the ability to attend a senior high school of choice as a central point of discussion. Public senior high schools are the cheapest, but also the most competitive, schools to get into. This means that financial constraints not only made private high schools and university unaffordable for students from low-income families but also added pressure to perform well on entrance exams, since entering a competitive public high school was the only option. In Tokunaga Asami's case, the impact of family finances on her education was particularly apparent, because her father's income was at a low point at the time she was about to enter senior high school. She bitterly notes:

> My older sister went to university because at the time, my parents still had enough money. But in my case, unless I got into [a highly competitive] public university, there was no need for me to go. And since I was not all that smart, I did not go to university.... My father only let me take exams for the municipal public senior high school, and although that was very risky and even my high school teacher recommended I should try at least one other one as a last resort, I was told that there was no money for that.

Tokunaga felt bitter about these foreclosed opportunities, frustrated that financial considerations rather than her merit and promise determined her future.

For Yoshida Megumi, whose mother received public assistance, the inability to apply for more than one senior high school seemed to require much less explanation: "Because my family was not that affluent, we couldn't afford to attend a private senior high school. I applied for one public senior high school but, because I failed the entrance exam, I went to an evening senior high school (*teijisei kôkô*), from 5 to 9 p.m." Low in fees, evening schools cater to children from families with very limited means, as they make it possible to work day jobs while completing senior high school and hence attract many students from low-income families. Where Tokunaga acutely felt a sense of injury in not being afforded the opportunities her sister enjoyed, Yoshida was resigned to the choices that seemed obvious for the child of a single mother receiving public assistance and, instead, felt proud of actually having completed her senior high school degree.

Limited family income also meant that those from low-income family backgrounds often started working as soon as they entered senior high school to finance the school tuition and to contribute to the household income. Yoshida Megumi started working a day job once she entered an evening high school in order to pay for school fees and to save for her driver's license. Although her days were long, she very much appreciated the personal income: finally she was able to afford a few personal items and dress up in fashionable clothing.

Women from two-parent households would also work if family finances were tight. Sakai Yoshimi notes:

> When I graduated from elementary school, my mother started working because they, of course, could not afford the fees to send us to university. So they told us to get a job. It was taken for granted that we would work, and that after senior high school you should get a job.... But senior high school also has tuition. So, from senior high school I started working part-time and paid my family. I worked at the cash register at the supermarket and sorted mail at the post office for two-and-a-half years. It's almost like I was mostly working. About five days a week, five to eight. After getting out of school, I went [to my job], and in the case of the supermarket I worked until eight. On the weekends, it was a little longer, from midday. It's hard to study [under such conditions]. And, actually, I don't think I really studied [for school]! Because I had the impression that I had to start working right after leaving high school, when I entered senior high school, in any case, I figured I just needed to get credits.

Sakai's family circumstances not only dictated that she would seek financial independence at an early age, but also clearly generated living conditions which stretched her ability to invest time and resources in acquiring qualifications or, for that matter, to pay much attention to her senior high school education to the limits. Her educational opportunities were not just foreclosed by her family's financial constraints but also living conditions which placed high demands on her time and energy, and made educational achievements no more than an afterthought. That is, although she knew she would need to pursue full-time work as an adult, there was insufficient space to consider working toward qualifications that might have improved her employment opportunities.

A family consisting of a father who works as a white-collar employee and a stay-at-home mother, therefore, was not necessarily a lifestyle limited to the middle-class. However, university and high school graduates were clearly positioned differently vis-à-vis the normative middle-class family ideal and developed different dispositions toward their future. Where women university graduates often took for granted that mothers stayed at home and that children would attend university, women from low-income families unable to afford a higher education saw the same ideal as an aspiration rather than a norm.

Where some university graduates felt pressured by their parents' ambitions for their educational future and barely gave a thought to their housing situation, financial situation, or professional future, high school graduates were clearly aware of their departure from the idealized lifestyle of a middle-class family life, marked by their residence in small apartments, lack of educational opportunities, and the need to contribute to the family income from an early age. Central to their understanding of class was, notably, not merely the occupation and income of fathers in white-collar employment, but also the living conditions, family lifestyle, and the educational aspirations that they could afford.

EMPLOYMENT AND CAREER IN THE BUBBLE ECONOMY

How women approached their future employment was, however, not just a question of educational credentials. Among both high school graduates and university graduates were women who consciously pursued a specific career trajectory as well as women who approached the labor market after graduation with little information, ambition, or direction. What mattered in defining their pathways to employment, therefore, was not only their educational attainment and qualifications, but also their personal disposition and their vision of their personal future.

Particularly high school graduates were often aware of the need to work as adults, whether single or married, leading some of them to make clear and informed choices about their future employment at an early stage. Some of these women who may be described as coming from a "settled living" background (Rubin 1976) appeared quite knowledgeable about their options and, furthermore, received concrete advice from their parents about possible qualifications and opportunities for employment. Kato Minako recalls:

> Since I was a child, I wanted to become a teacher at a day care center, but I ended up going out [instead of studying] during high school. And I heard it was hard to get that kind of job because it is a popular job. So I talked about getting a job with my mother, and about getting a qualification such as for hairdressing or nursing. I decided to get a qualification. Nursing, I was afraid of what it would involve, so that's how I decided to become a hair dresser.

Where senior high school graduates in the 1960s and 1970s felt that employment opportunities were in abundance, Kato's reflections underscore the importance of specific qualifications and female employment niches as a means to find stable employment as a high school graduate from the Bubble generation.

But where Kato attended a professional school after graduation from senior high school to obtain her training, this was not an option for everyone.

In Sakai Yoshimi's case, for example, the costs of professional training further limited her options. She recounts:

> When I was little, I wanted to take a qualification as a teacher at a day care center. But in those days, if you were not able to play the piano, you could not become a teacher. So I was told, because that is impossible, I should let go [of the idea]. I was soon persuaded. Something like piano, you can't master it if you don't get to study it.... So I said, "Alright, I see," and I agreed to give up the idea.

Unable to afford the necessary schooling for the qualification, Sakai pursued general office work without additional training after graduation.

However, it was not only finances but also access to information and advice about employment that appeared to make a difference. Where Kato and Sakai discussed specific options with their parents, others approached their future in a rather haphazard fashion without guidance from parents or peers. Kimura Eiko, for instance, did not appear to consult her parents about her future and she dropped out of senior high school only to realize that she could not get a job without a senior high school degree. She recalls:

> When you look for work, even for a part-time job, you need to have graduated at least from senior high school. That's what I realized after I quit school. Maybe I actually liked school, even if I hated going. I then went to a vocational school. You could learn how to become a telephone operator. But even for that you would need to have a senior high school degree, so I decided to go back to an evening school.

Unaware of the consequences of failing to complete her senior high school degree, she returned to school to pursue a qualification she hoped would provide her with better employment prospects.

In other cases, women were clearly aware of the need to work, but had little idea of how to maximize their potential, despite ample work experience. Yoshida Megumi, for instance, worked in a local supermarket at the cash register as a senior high school student but, after graduation from senior high school, saw little reason to move beyond that position. "The salary was pretty good," she said. "That's why I thought it's not necessary to get a real [permanent] job, also because I was staying with my family." Having felt the pinch of limited family finances as a teenager, she felt comfortable with her income from part-time work, with which she could contribute to household finances while also having some money left for her personal consumption. In other words, "work," for Yoshida, was a matter of "income." What exactly a permanent contract was and how having a permanent contract differed from being a part-time employee were not clear to her until much later in life. While this lack of knowledge and foresight about her employment future may not have had as much of an impact during the period of high-speed economic growth, when full-time employment, including for high school graduates, was common, the onset of the recession and the rise in unstable employment among high school graduates in the 1990s made a more strategic approach to employment of increasing importance.

For university graduates from the Bubble generation, employment opportunities appeared more plentiful, but the possibilities for long-term employment shortly after the introduction of the Equal Employment Opportunities Law still remained limited. Unlike high school graduates, moreover, few expected to work for the long-term, despite expanding opportunities. Mori Asako, a university graduate who witnessed the shifts following the introduction of the EEOL, explains: "When I graduated from university, the EEOL had just begun.... I realized that if you get a job, you have to work overtime and more overtime, and all you do is work. I thought it was a real waste.... At the time, it was common to quit upon marriage even if you had a permanent job."

As full-time employment often took the form of such menial jobs as those of Office Ladies (Ogasawara 1998), there was also little incentive to stay employed. Kawasaki Mariko, for instance, found her first job in the second year of the Equal Employment Opportunities Law. Nevertheless, she felt relegated to the usual gendered tasks: pouring tea, making photocopies, writing reports. She notes: "I arrived at work at 8:30 in the morning. We would get the papers and prepare tea—green tea, Oolong tea, coffee, Genmai tea." She not only had to serve tea in the morning, at lunch time, and in the evening, leaving little time for her own work, but also had to remember who preferred what and when. She also had difficulties with her superior and, feeling stressed, she would go out to drink until late at night. Eventually she collapsed from the overloaded lifestyle only half a year into her job. Her difficulties with her work relations could be considered a matter of her own character; yet they also reflected the contradictory position in which she found herself. She was eager to become independent and to work full-time, but felt frustrated by the menial tasks and subordinate role she was assigned. Eventually, she found an office job in a non-profit organization, which provided her a greater level of responsibility and independence.

There was however also a small number of women who worked in the public sector or in traditional feminized professions such as school teaching, or had professional qualifications, in particular clerical accounting, who enjoyed more stable and long-term employment opportunities. Notably, not all of them had planned for or anticipated a long-term working career. Obuchi Miho, for example, started out without particular plans for long-term employment, but was able to find well-paying and stable employment as a qualified clerical accountant at a later stage. She recalls:

> After graduation [from junior college], I had no idea of what to do. I had no specific goal.... I did not know what to do. I thought about perhaps doing further studies, but I had not worked hard during college. I had just hung around and had not looked for work. But in the end, after I graduated, [my friends] had already gotten selected for a job but, in my case, nothing had been decided.

Eventually, Obuchi found a job in advertising. Yet the initial attraction quickly wore off. She soon realized that her actual task was that of an intermediary and that it was bureaucratic rather than creative in nature, offering few rewards. In addition, being unmarried as she reached her thirties meant that her priorities and outlook on employment changed. Facing the prospect of remaining unmarried, she received advice from friends and colleagues on how to stay employed above age thirty. She recounts:

> When I was getting older, I did not know what I wanted to do, but someone, a friend, suggested it would be better for me to get some qualifications.... I did bookkeeping at work. I was not good at it, but I took the qualification anyway.... I tried working in advertising and other flashy employment sectors but, in the end, I am not a person with great skills, so I thought, "Why not?"

Although Obuchi had not planned on long-term employment and, if anything, had been largely unsure about how to pursue her employment future, the acquisition of a professional qualification as a clerical accountant—a skill in which she had little confidence—ended up offering her employment stability and a good wage even above the age of forty.

Despite considerable advances in educational attainment and the expansion of employment opportunities, full-time career-track employment for most women thus appeared the exception rather than the rule. For high school graduates, finding stable employment without a university degree became more difficult than for the previous generation, requiring strategic investment in particular qualifications to ensure more stable employment. For junior college graduates as well, qualifications, even if acquired at a later stage, became an important means of ensuring long-term employment, particularly when they became too old for regular clerical jobs. University graduates, in turn, experienced the fewest obstacles in finding employment upon graduation, but often had work experiences that offered them few prospects for the future and were not a source of status and identity. The question this all posed, then, was not simply whether women were eager to invest in and commit themselves to a career, but also how women might negotiate their personal future between marriage, motherhood, and employment.

Chapter 3
CHRISTMAS CAKES AND LOSER DOGS

How did the Bubble generation approach the idea of marriage and motherhood? In light of the lack, in most cases, of a clear sense of place or fulfillment in the world of work, it may not be entirely surprising that marriage and motherhood was perceived as at least offering a sense of identity and social achievement. After all, women from the Bubble generation grew up with the ideal of the salaryman family that evoked a timely marriage and the role of the housewife as an achievement and source of social status and identity. Tanaka Miyuki's view of marriage offers a characteristic description of the ideal life course.

> Personally, I really aspired to marriage. When I was that age, there was the idea of Christmas cake. Until twenty-four sells, twenty-five sells okay, twenty-six does not sell. That was the silent assumption. My parents and I thought I should marry early. Many thought that to marry and become a good wife meant happiness. I wanted to become a good wife and have children, and form a happy household.

Tanaka belonged to a small elite of women who had access to an exclusive private-school education and a university degree at an elite university, which, however, was not considered as the starting point for a working career. Fond of children, she married someone working for a large corporation shortly after completing her bachelor's degree and, since her husband's company did not encourage the employment of spouses, she became a full-time housewife.

Even if women were not quite as enthusiastic about becoming full-time housewives as Tanaka, the expectation of a timely marriage and standardized life course leading up to married motherhood made a regular appearance in many stories of young adulthood. As women reached their late twenties without getting married, the timing of marriage, in particular, became a central point of concern. Kondo Naoko, who worked full-time in a challenging job, and enjoyed her good work relations, for example, explains:

> I was twenty-six, or twenty-seven. In my late twenties, before I turned thirty, I increasingly felt pressured. My friends, those of the same age as me, they were fast, they were already married then. There is this term, *kekkon tekireiki* [appropriate time to get married]. When you turn twenty-six or twenty-seven, there is this feeling that it is time to get married. My parents also thought that way, and I myself would worry, "Am I going to turn thirty just like that?" That's what I started thinking about. I thought I should do something about it before then. It was a burning issue for me.

Kondo was part of the generation that had greater access to career-track jobs which offered challenges and personal development. Nevertheless, in approaching age thirty, the urge to get married and settle came to outweigh her professional goals. Anticipating marriage, she quit her job to be able to travel and reflect, and married soon after her return. She explains:

> He had been my lover for a very short time, but I thought it would work out. So at the age of twenty-eight, I thought it is about time, and I did not work anywhere as a full-time employee at the time. I hadn't planned to look for work and work full-time again. I also did not want to continue to live with my parents.... So I said, "Let's get married!"

Marriage, in this case, appeared as an important milestone for reaching social adulthood and gaining independence from her parental home, where she had continued to reside after graduation from university. In addition, it was not just age, but also often the wish to become a mother, that played a role in women's eagerness to marry. Kawasaki Mariko, who also married in her late twenties, illustrates this connection. In a rush to get married before the age of thirty, she decided to marry a long-term on-and-off boyfriend without being herself very convinced of the relationship. As she relates:

> Things did not go well before we got married. Even my parents advised me to end the relationship, but I really wanted a child. It would take time to have a child, and searching for another partner. So we went abroad for a small-scale wedding. We had the typical experience of having arguments on our honeymoon, but [instead of a "Narita" divorce upon return to the airport from the honeymoon] I decided to stay quiet until having a baby, and to bear with the marriage until a child was born.... Because I wanted children, it didn't matter with whom, I just wanted to marry.

Marriage, here, merely appears as a means to an end—to facilitate motherhood and confirm a woman's social status in line with a standardized life course of the postwar Japanese family system and to escape the risky status of the unmarried single woman or "loser dog" (Kanbara 1991; Sakai 2003).

The idea of marriage and motherhood as an aspiration and sign of social adulthood was also present in the stories of high school graduates. Kato Minako echoes earlier comments about marriage:

> When I was twenty-four or twenty-five, I really wanted to get married. It was also that kind of age, my friends got married, I felt this social pressure. There is that social assumption [that you should get married]. I was really amazed by marriage. I aspired to marriage, and I really wanted to get married. But when I was twenty-four and twenty-five, there was nobody [I could have married]. I was unlucky. But I knew my husband since high school. We were together for about ten years, so when I was twenty-seven, we got married.

Similarly to Kondo, Kato felt pressured to get married "on time," as her friends were getting married one after another. Notably, although she had not considered her husband as a suitable partner when she was in her midtwenties (as she said, there was "nobody"), he had become a realistic option in her late twenties. Marriage, here too, appeared as a means to the end of achieving social adulthood and of being able to become a mother.

Motherhood was also central to high school graduates' descriptions of a happy family life. Matsui Shigeko, for instance, articulated her aspirations toward marriage as follows:

> With regard to marriage, I thought I wanted to have a lot of children. I was imagining a happy and lively family. So when I got pregnant, I thought, well, I would like to have about six more [children]. Until then, I had been working all the time. But I also wanted children—not exactly seven—even though I also wanted to continue working. That was my ideal home, with many children, and someone I get along with. So when we separated, it was a bit of a shock.... But even now, I think I would like to have a lot of children. I would like to have a family, with children at the center. For some time, I guess it will be just the two of us. Marriage, I thought, was fun. And I am really happy that I had the child. Now, we pass every day happily.

Matsui had lived independently from her parents, and worked to support herself since she was a teenager, yet she saw no contradiction between her employment and aspirations to motherhood. Underscoring the centrality of motherhood to married women's identity, Matsui also effortlessly conflated marriage with motherhood, responding to a question about marriage with her enthusiasm about becoming a mother.

But as high school graduates, on average, married at a somewhat younger age, there were also other considerations that accompanied their approach to marriage. To begin with, some considered marriage an important source of economic stability as well as social mobility. Sakai Yoshimi, for example, had worked since high school and had rented her own apartment while working in a stable office job. Yet, she was aware that, as a single woman, she would not be able to afford a standard middle-class lifestyle. As she describes:

> Around me, middle-class people were having a nice life but I lived in an apartment without a bath.... At that time, someone asked me to get married. He promised I could become a professional housewife, so that I could take care of my parents during the day [without having to work]. We could rent an apartment nearby so that I could take care of my parents.... How about that? I said, "Yes!" and we got married.

Between the demands of work to support herself and the care of her ageing parents, marriage emerged as an attractive means to attain a more comfortable lifestyle. Sakai not only felt that marriage was an important means of attaining a higher standard of living, but having worked full-time since she was a teenager, she also saw becoming a full-time housewife and being able to care for her parents as an attractive prospect for a stable and secure lifestyle.

For women who had taken for granted that they would be working even in marriage, the ability to stay at home could also be viewed as a luxury rather than a constraint. Kato Minako, who pursued specific qualifications already as a teenager in anticipation of life-long employment, noted: "Personally, if there was a husband who would support me, I would prefer staying home, even though I am not a very homey person. Probably I am just lazy." Staying at home rather than working as a mother, for Kato, appeared as a sign of comfort that would allow her to avoid a hard life of balancing work and family life. Kimura Eiko, who lived in a public housing unit with her husband, also thought it would be best if she stayed at home with the children once married, despite their limited household income. Achieving a "normal" family life for high school graduates from low-income families, therefore, was not necessarily just a matter of conformity but could also symbolize a certain level of comfort and a form of social mobility and achievement.

But even though high school graduates made reference to the dominant middle-class ideal of family in talking about marriage, their understanding of the normative ideal of family differed. Kimura Eiko describes her image of marriage and having a family: "My dream of marriage was very normal. I had the image of marriage as sitting in a sunlit room with my spouse and children, watching TV, having fun. That is what I aspired to. My mother and father were very normal people and they are still getting along. I thought that was normal and I also wanted to become like that."

Yoshida Megumi, likewise, emphasized partnership as an important element of her image of a happy family life. She remembers:

> I thought we [my partner and I] would be like friends, and pass every day together happily. I wanted to have a normal family. And on the weekends, we would all go somewhere by car. And once the children are grown up, when we are grandma and grandpa, we would still walk hand-in-hand, passing every day together happily. That's what I dreamed of.

While Kimura and Yoshida's aspirations of a happy family life and intimate partnership may not strike one as particularly unusual, they stood in stark contrast to earlier accounts of university graduates, who focused on the achievement of a timely marriage and in whose accounts partnership in marriage and conjugal relations made only scarce appearances.

Also their motivations as mothers differed. Kimura Eiko, for instance, took issue with the fact that she had grown up with a working mother. Having felt lonely on returning to an empty home after school, she was determined to be there for her children as a married wife and mother. She explains: "If I work, I worry about not being able to properly look after my children." "Being there," for Kimura, meant, in particular, being able to give her children a place to let off steam after they returned from school. Rather than being focused on being an education mother, her concerns focused on her personal experience of loneliness due to the absence from home of her working mother. Even Kato, who had always been enthusiastic about having children and had had ambitions to become a kindergarten teacher, noted her dream of staying at home: "I don't think it would make a difference in raising my child." Being a stay-at-home mother, in these cases, was about the ability to avoid the drudgeries of working motherhood and to spend time with their children. It seems remote from the high demands on housewives and mothers that are central to the lives of many middle-class mothers (Ehara 2000).

The stories of women from the Bubble generation, in this way, highlight the central presence of the postwar ideal of the salaryman and the full-time housewife and mother in defining the meaning and significance of marriage and motherhood, particularly for middle-class women's life trajectories. Marriage, motherhood, and the role of housewife and mother in these stories appear not simply as life events and gender roles, but more often seem understood as crucial milestones that confer a sense of social attainment and recognition, in conformity with the expected life course of a middle-class woman. There were also, of course, differences in women's interpretations of this ideal. Whereas some university graduates seemed particularly concerned about adherence to the ideal so as to be able to confirm their status as middle-class women by means of a timely marriage and motherhood, high school graduates often hoped for a life beyond the hardships of their own upbringing, underscoring the status and comfort associated with becoming a housewife and mother.

ALTERNATIVE PERSPECTIVES

There were, certainly, also women who held a more critical stance toward the institution of marriage and the idealized life course of a married housewife and mother. A small number of university graduates who, notably, enjoyed a higher level of economic independence were among those who showed less concern about adherence to the norm and instead pursued alternatives to the conventional salaryman family and standardized life course of the married housewife and mother. While not opposed to marriage or having children per se, they represent a growing critique of the institutionalized model of marriage among the women of this generation.

Yoshioka Rie's story offers an illustrative example. Raised by a mother who encouraged her to embrace the equal rights and opportunities promised to women by the postwar Japanese constitution, she was eager to pursue a profession and long-term career after graduating from university. When she married in her mid-twenties, she took for granted that their relationship would be guided by a sense of equality. "I thought that in marriage, partners should be independent and self-sufficient.... We were friends from university and we got married when I was in my mid-twenties." Both Yoshioka and her husband pursued their professions full-time, which did not pose an issue initially. However, when she remained involuntarily childless for a few years into their marriage, she felt increasingly pressured to quit her job and become a mother. "There was this term called DINKS (double income, no kids). We were part of that generation. I thought, 'Well, if I have children, that's fine,' but I thought it did not have to happen right now." Happy in her job and leading a comfortable life in Tokyo, she saw no immediate need to pressure herself into becoming a mother.

But, as she remained childless even in her late twenties, the topic of children became an increasing source of tension. She recounts:

> His family started asking, "When are you going to have children?" They really pressured me. Now that I think about it, I think I just got very nervous. I felt cornered. Whenever we went to his parents, they asked: "When are you going to have children? Are you not going to stop working?" [Even my husband] said that if I quit working and stayed home, I would be able to have children. But I said that even if I have children, I want to continue working.

Although Yoshioka did not in principle resist the idea of marriage or motherhood (and eventually did have a child), the pressure and criticism she faced as a married woman made her increasingly critical of the institution of marriage. She came to realize that the expectation to quit work and become a mother was much more present in her immediate environment than she had thought, and she felt exposed and objectified by the discussion of the subject.

> I was married for three years by then, but I did not have children. So they thought I might have a problem and should go and find out at the hospital. They started talking about that in regular conversation. Even my husband's superior at work seems to have said that. Japan is like that. It makes me shudder to think that this kind of language was being used. You must be kidding—his boss at work does not even know me.... I became really depressed. My friends, in my thirties, they all had children. My mother, as I said before, she tried not to pressure me that way. She said I should not worry about it. Even toward my mother, I felt guilty in the course of all of this. A married woman who cannot have children. What a loser!

Yoshioka's story visualizes not only the continuing pressure to conform to a prescribed life course of a timely marriage and motherhood, but also how she herself, despite her economic independence and progressive upbringing, had difficulties disassociating herself from such a view. Once she had reached her thirties and was married, her educational and professional achievements, as argued by Sakai (2003), could not replace motherhood as a primary means to assert a married woman's identity.

Yoshioka, however, did find a source of support in her acquaintance with the movement for separate last names (*fûfû bessei*), which explicitly rejects marriage as an institution but not as a practice (Yoshizumi 1997). Under the family registration system, which governs marriage and family relations in Japan, the key unit of personal identification is not the individual (as in the case of a driver's license or social security number in the United States), but the nuclear family, meaning that family relations are included in personal identification records. Women leave their parents' family record upon marriage and enter the family record of their husbands as dependents (unless husbands decide to join their wives' record) when they register their marriage. Marriage, therefore, does not merely consist of a contract between individuals but is a means by which a woman joins her husband's family unit.

As Yoshizumi's (1997) research has shown, couples who live in common-law marriages (without completing official marriage papers) reject legal marriage because it assumes a hierarchical relationship between husband and wife—literally making wives dependents of husbands in the family registration record—and implies a traditional division of labor in the home. Yet, although they do not register their marriages, they live together as if legally married and consider each other husband and wife. Mostly highly educated, these couples also tend to have significantly more progressive views of gender roles in the family. Asked about how couples manage differences in opinion, few women in common-law marriages agree that they should abide by their husband's opinion, even though 71.5% of women in legal marriages do so. Men in common-law marriages also tend to be significantly more involved in housework and child-rearing (Yoshizumi 1997, 133ff). As the numbers of such marriages are not within statistical grasp, it needs to be kept in mind that such views represent a phenomenon of a small minority rather than a large-scale trend.

Yoshioka's attempt to convince her partner to pursue the idea of "separate last names"—in practice, unregistering their marriage—failed. While she considered this approach a means of equalizing and modernizing their relationship by disassociating herself from the family registration system, her spouse saw it as a proposal to divorce. Yoshioka's struggles illustrate the close connection of the institution of marriage with particular gender roles and expectations. If marriage has been institutionalized in the form of a family headed by a male breadwinner, with women's role as a mother and housewife, the movement of common-law marriages indicates that marriage, as institutionalized by the family registration system, is no longer considered by some to be a suitable frame for more innovative and equal forms of spousal and family relations.

This approach was also taken by Imamura Naoko, who lived in a common-law marriage when becoming a mother. Surrounded by a progressive community and working as a freelancer, she took for granted that marriage was not necessary for entering an intimate and long-term commitment. She recounts her first encounter with her partner and their subsequent relationship:

> I was working at a small company. That is when I met him, and I immediately thought I would like to be together with him…. He was working a lot overseas, and I myself had traveled abroad a lot when I was a student, and I was interested in exploring new places. So I continued my work as a freelancer while traveling with him.

Even though she was in her late twenties when she became pregnant, she did not insist on formalizing their relationship. As she explains, "[When I found out that I was pregnant], we thought one does not have to insist on registering the marriage … so we did not formally get married. When the baby was born, he officially declared his paternity." Imamura not only happily rejected norms and regulations about marriage but, in line with Yoshizumi's (1997) findings, was also among the few to articulate an alternative view of marital relationships. In contrast to accounts previously discussed, she was also among the few actually to discuss her conjugal relationship and partner. Where spouses appeared as a mere means to achieve the status of a married wife and mother in other stories, Imamura clearly saw her relationship with her partner as an important element of her personal life.

Notably, neither Yoshioka nor Imamura were opposed to the idea of a long-term commitment to a spouse or, for that matter, to the possibility of becoming a mother. Rather, their approaches reflect a critique of the unequal marital relationships implied and institutionalized by the family registration system and the postwar ideal of the salaryman family.

Their views however also need to be considered within their economic context. As self-sufficient university graduates with good employment prospects and incomes, well read and grown up in progressive families, these women possessed a range of resources, and were in a unique position to explore the possibility of alternative marriage arrangements. In light of women's more general continuing economic dependence on a breadwinner to be able not only to make ends meet but also to uphold a middle-class living standard (Raymo and Ishikawa 2005), their experience was the exception rather than the rule.

PERSPECTIVES ON DIVORCE

Of course, since most single mothers are divorcees, a critical stance toward the institution of marriage may not be limited to those who avoid registering their marriage. At the same time, the fact that divorced single mothers of this generation did get married and become mothers at a time when marriage is on the decline and fertility levels have dropped also means that the experiences of these women can offer important insights into the growing challenges of pursuing a normative life course, from a timely marriage to a lifestyle as a housewife and mother. That is, while divorcees are often assumed to symbolize a decline in adherence to traditional marriage norms, the gender division of labor and women's role as mothers were not actually the most central topics they raised when they discussed their marriages. More often, in fact, it was the failure of their partners to conform to the normative ideal of the male breadwinner that caused friction. That is, while divorce did make them critical of the institution of marriage, many explained the reasons for their divorce as a consequence of the inability to achieve a "normal" family life and as an extension of their role as responsible mothers.

Tanaka Miyuki, who pursued a picture-book life course with an elite education and marriage to a businessman with a high income, for example, had embraced the idea of becoming a housewife and mother but found herself empty and at a loss as her marriage remained childless years after getting married. As she reflects:

> I thought that to continue like this would not be good for me. I was not able to have children. I really wanted children, and made many inquiries but was told by his mother that "the problem was probably with the woman." I started thinking about what marriage is really about. When I turned thirty, I started thinking about a lot of things. If there were no children, I wondered what I would do in the future, and what I had lived for.

Tanaka stayed faithful to her partner for many years, putting up with excessive drinking and debts. When she finally decided to end the relationship because of her frustrations about her childlessness, her family—which had expected her to marry early and forego a working career—sighed with relief. "My family was happy to hear that," she said. "They knew I was bearing with it for a long time." Tanaka's divorce, in other words, was not motivated by her demands for change, but rather by her wish to fulfill her aspiration of becoming a mother.

As husbands were expected to provide for the family as breadwinners, unemployment and debts also frequently featured in mothers' stories about divorce. Women married to high school graduates, in particular, were often faced with their husband's unstable employment, reflective of the increasingly difficult employment opportunities after the collapse of the Bubble economy and the growth of irregular employment particularly among high school graduates during this time period. Yushima Kayoko, a junior college graduate whose husband worked in a construction firm explained:

> When I was seven months pregnant [with our second child], my husband had trouble at work and did not go anymore. He had stopped working for a month or so at the time before, so I thought he would soon go back, given that there are the children to take care of. But in the end, he did not go back [to work], which was the main reason for our divorce.

Yushima had worked for a number of years before getting married, but at her husband's request had quit her job. "He said, 'We can make it with my salary, please quit your job.'" Yet, his attempt to become the sole breadwinner of the family and earn respect as a husband failed miserably, as he could not get along with colleagues and did not make an attempt to pursue other work. Frustrated about his situation, he also became violent toward his family. Yushima remembers:

> He drank quite a lot, became stressed, and started to become violent toward the children.... He had no place to let off his stress, so he bullied the children.... It would not be good for the children, for myself as well, to continue living like that. Under these circumstances, divorce was the only option.

For Yushima, it was, therefore, not the gender division of labor and expectation of becoming a housewife, but rather her husband's inability and apparent unwillingness to provide for his family, along with the threat of domestic violence and concern for the welfare of her children, that led her to leave their relationship and seek refuge in a domestic violence shelter.

Kato Minako, likewise, felt forced to divorce her husband because of mounting debts and his literal absence from a shared family life. As she describes:

> After we got married, I realized he was into *pachinko* [pinball games].... I knew he did it sometimes, but he really liked it.... He played every night until the store closed around ten or eleven. He no longer came home for dinner; I waited at the beginning, but because I got hungry, I ended up eating by myself. So it was like living by myself. I wondered, "Is this what it means to get married?" We are not fighting, but since I am cooking by myself and eating by myself, it is like living by myself. I was very lonely. I thought this is not what a marriage is supposed to be like. I didn't like to scold him, and at the beginning, I didn't think that doing *pachinko* has a bad effect on others. It did not really obstruct our daily life. It was a hobby—that's what I thought. But it seems like he used up a lot of money at the *pachinko* parlor. He took out loans with seven loan companies, for about ¥2 million (US$18,182). In the end, he no longer gave me any money for our living expenses—this is how our living conditions went downhill.

Faced with debts and calls from moneylenders, she continued working throughout her pregnancy and after giving birth to her daughter, but, as conditions did not improve, even her parents agreed that she might do better without a husband. Kato Minako explained her decision to leave him:

> I actually did not want to divorce. It is not just about appearances, but I did not want to make our child the child of a single parent. I thought if we separate, the child would face the prejudice of being the child of a single mother. There are these prejudices. People say, "Because the mother is a single parent...." It is an old story.... In any case, I thought it was normal to have two parents—it was like that for me. I thought, "Why should I make her life so difficult?" But, then, I wondered how children feel about growing up with parents who argue all the time. It might be better to grow up in a happy household than with arguing parents.

Not only did Kato have difficulties considering a lifestyle outside of the nuclear family norm, her child's future also weighed heavily in her consideration of divorce. Rather than abandoning family values, Kato explained her motivation to divorce based on her wish to be a good parent and have a financially stable family life.

Divorce was thus not necessarily a result of a critical stance toward the institution of marriage per se, but rather may be explained as a consequence of the contradictory realities women came to face during marriage. Infidelity, unemployment, debts, addiction, and domestic violence are also the most cited reasons for judicial divorces (Japan High Court 2012). If motherhood is most central to the idea of marriage, it can also become a justification for divorce when marriage is no longer considered a feasible environment for child-rearing. Rather than having been critical of marriage from the beginning, it was often the inability to rely on a male breadwinner to support them and their children that made these women consider divorce. Faced with an economy that made it increasingly difficult for high-school educated men to secure a stable job and income, the high incidence of economic troubles and higher share of less educated women among single mothers (Fujiwara 2007) yet again highlight the close relationship between the economy and marriage.

"UNMARRIED" MOTHERS

Unmarried mothers, likewise, were not necessarily opposed to the possibility of marriage. As Ekaterina Hertog (2009) has shown in her study of unmarried single mothers, giving birth outside of marriage is not necessarily an indication of a woman's rejection of marriage, but can also indicate a "failure" of their potential marriages. Her research also underscores the centrality of the aspiration of a middle-class, normative family life and belief that a two-parent family is the ideal setting for parenting as the reason why so few women give birth outside of marriage. Unmarried mothers are, therefore, not necessarily forerunners of family change but, like divorcees, allow insight into the growing contradictions and tensions surrounding marriage and family in contemporary Japan.

Like divorcees, unmarried mothers in this study also often evoked quite conventional aspirations of motherhood when narrating their stories of youth and young adulthood. In some cases, women became unmarried single mothers precisely because they assumed—like many divorcees—that marriage meant becoming a mother. The story of Matsui Shigeko, whom we heard enthusiastically speak about the prospect of marriage and having a lively family with many children earlier, reflects this idea. She discusses the events that led to the birth of her daughter as follows:

> We started going out and decided to marry, but then I found out he already had children. I didn't know that then. He was [from another prefecture] and was working in Tokyo for one of his company's branch offices. We had lived together for one year.... We were just about to register the marriage and fix the wedding date.... So, with that in mind, I became pregnant. But shortly before giving birth, I learnt about all of this.... I made a lot of inquiries and, in the end, [his wife] found out that I am expecting a baby. I am not sure about the details but she seems to have attempted suicide; he didn't say anything specific. So, therefore, he did not separate [from his wife] and I ended up separating from him.

According to recent statistics, as many as a quarter of first-born children in Japan are conceived before marriage (MHLW 2004). Matsui's expectation that her relationship would become formalized in marriage, particularly after getting pregnant, was in this sense not unusual, yet instead, it led her to become an unmarried single mother.

There were also women who had no plans to get married, but decided to keep a child after finding themselves unexpectedly pregnant. Yoshioka Rie's experience provides an illustrative example. Divorced after a childless marriage, she had reconciled herself to a life as a single and childless woman, having had difficulties conceiving during her marriage. Faced with an unplanned pregnancy and a boyfriend with whom she got along but had no intention to marry, she considered her options.

> Maybe it was fate. At forty-one, [I realized I was pregnant]. I was shocked. At thirty-five, it is called "late childbearing" (*kôrei shussan*) but at forty? I had never seen anyone who had given birth at forty.... I no longer had the dream of having a family, or marrying. I figured there would be relatives who would give me a hard time. It would be better to go out with the person I like, to be free.... But then I got pregnant. It was so unusual. I was forty, and I had not really thought about raising a child.... But I was with my back to the wall—no

way out. If I let this chance go, I would never have another child. If I searched for another partner, I figured I would be fifty. Now is the chance. I figured it would work out somehow. Once I got pregnant, things changed, it was an eventful year. I said, "I will have it whatever the cost!"

One of the characteristics Yoshioka shared with several other women who gave birth outside of marriage is that she found herself pregnant at the outer limits of childbearing age in their mid-thirties to early forties. Where those seeking marriage felt thirty was the magic age and the "last chance," unexpectedly pregnant women in their mid- to late thirties similarly felt this was the last, though not necessarily ideal, chance to have a child.

The prospect of becoming a mother also promised to add meaning and purpose to sometimes uneventful lives. Kaneko Yoshimi, for instance, had an unsuccessful working career and, in her thirties, the prospect of not having children seemed even more daunting than remaining unmarried. She recalls:

> In my thirties, I started thinking that I wanted to give birth, and wanted a child. That feeling became stronger. And even my mother thought, "Even if you can't marry, you can have a child." I don't think she foresaw this, but she sort of said, "If only you had a child...." She thought it would be a good thing.... Because she had said that, I thought somehow she would help me out [when I found myself pregnant]. I thought she would understand. She said that if you want to have it that badly, all sort of things had happened before that. So she said, "It's fine." This really helped me. There are others who are kicked out by their parents. But in my case, my mother was there for me.

Kaneko did not have exceptionally strong views about marriage and had felt unlucky and powerless in coping with her life so far. Facing a bleak future without a partner or a rewarding job, having a child was for her—and interestingly also for her mother—a unique means to find a purpose in life.

This sentiment was echoed by others who had gone through the experience of marriage and divorce but had not quite given up on the idea of becoming a mother. Obuchi Miho notes:

> After getting divorced, I thought I would not want to go through that again, so I could not bring myself to think positively about remarriage. But I wanted a child. Even if I don't get married, I wanted a child. I think this is how I felt. That was in my thirties.... Because I wanted to have a child, I was very happy about [finding myself pregnant]. When I realized I was pregnant, I was very happy. I thought I would raise it by myself. That was really big. I happened to be with my parents. I was hoping my mother would help me, and I would work for this company. There was nobody who had taken a maternity leave before, but after giving birth, if I could continue [working], I would have an income. I did not know how much a child would cost, but I thought I could somehow make it.

Obuchi earned a decent salary but was aware of the challenges of working and supporting herself and a child as a single mother. Rather than a career-track job or financial independence, it was the lack of a sense of accomplishment that made having a child attractive. As Kaneko explains, "It may sound strange, but for me, the first thing I really did well was to give birth.... That's what I think. It is self-centered to think about it this way, but for me, to have given birth, for me it was the thing I have done best." Rather than illustrating their economic independence, their life courses reveal a sense of limited opportunities and motherhood as a unique space in which to find a sense of personal accomplishment and affection, not unlike observations made elsewhere of unmarried mothers (Edin and Kefalas 2005).

If motherhood is the most central element of being a married woman, unmarried mothers can be considered to have embraced motherhood in the absence of a feasible marriage in which to pursue the role of mother. Tanaka Miyuki, who had dreamt of becoming a stereotypical housewife and mother, reflects on giving birth unmarried after a childless marriage:

> Well, in the end, I love children, so to have a lot of children around means happiness to me. Now, because I have my child, she is my strong support. As compared to that, I think even if I was still the wife of a famous businessman, probably my heart would be empty. Unfortunately, there is no man I can rely on!

If the love of children led her to aspire to marriage, it was also the dedication to becoming a mother in the absence of a husband who would fulfill his role that led her to become a single mother.

In contrast with women's stories from the pre-Bubble generation, the accounts of women of the Bubble generation highlight the centrality of the married-mother norm in their considerations of their life course and personal future. In the heyday of the ideal of the salaryman family and the full-time housewife, the role of the married wife and mother came to constitute more than a gender role and came to be treated as a milestone and social achievement that confirm a woman's social status and identity. As the working world offered few rewards, the recognition and respect afforded to married mothers made getting married and becoming a mother all the more appealing.

Yet, despite this eagerness to embrace motherhood and marriage, single mothers' life trajectories also illustrate the trials of marriage and having a family at a time when expectations and realities of marital life increasingly clashed. While they may have been impatient in putting up with an unhappy marriage, it was often breadwinners who, in their view, failed to deliver and concern over the welfare of their children that led them to separate from their spouses. Rather than having been skeptical about marriage from the beginning, many began to question the institution of marriage only once confronted with the pressures and contradictions of becoming a married wife and mother. In their pursuit of marriage and motherhood, single mothers did not necessarily resist existing family norms, but rather came to subvert them by taking them at face value. The continuing emphasis on a gender division of labor and on women's role as mother and homemaker has heightened the expectation that men should be reliable breadwinners and has made the presence of fathers and husbands, except for their economic role, of decreasing importance to women's visions of a happy family life. Rather than a reflection of women's growing economic independence, their stories highlight the increasing tensions and contradictions in family life and the growing difficulties of attaining and maintaining a family's economic security based on the reliance on a breadwinning husband, as envisioned by the postwar ideal of the salaryman family.

Chapter Four

Becoming a Single Mother

The experience of becoming a single mother, needless to say, came with challenges on many levels. Often, women literally had to start over from scratch, having to look for a new home and to find employment in order to rebuild their lives together with their children. Yet, their search for a place to live as a single mother not only marked a new life stage in the form of a new home and a fresh start. The challenges they encountered in looking for a suitable residence also revealed the specific conditions they came to face as single mothers in Japanese society. Mothers' employment trajectories, likewise, shed light not only on the challenges of combining the role of breadwinner and mother, but also on the consequences for single mothers of pursuing a lifestyle outside of the normative ideal of the married mother and male breadwinner household.

A NEW PLACE

For many mothers, one of the most immediate consequences of separation from a partner was the need to move house. According to a 2003 study, over 70% of single mothers change housing after becoming a single mother (JIL 2003). Also a dominant majority of mothers I interviewed had to find a new place to live upon separation. In most cases, it was mothers rather than their partners who left the shared residence upon separation, taking the children with them. A number of women felt forced to leave because of debts, gambling, and/or domestic violence. In other cases, women cited irreconcilable differences, often related to men's affairs, as the reason for separating from and leaving their partner. This predominance of mothers, rather than fathers, leaving the home after the end of a relationship not only highlights the severity of the circumstances under which many came to separate, but also underscores the idea that marriage is associated with women's entry into their husband's household (visualized by the *koseki* family registration system) and that, in turn, the end of a conjugal relation is interpreted as a woman's departure from her husband's household.

The need to move house could however also be a result of their new status as a divorcee or single mother. Yonekawa Sachiko, for example, divorced her spouse when her son was one-year-old but remained on friendly terms with her ex-husband. Although her ex-spouse left the apartment to her to keep, she was forced to look for a new place after being told by her landlords that they had "rented the apartment to a married, not a divorced, couple." Unmarried mothers were more likely to experience continuity in keeping their house and belongings, but the birth of a child could also complicate affairs. Matsui Shigeko, who had lived in a rented apartment with her boyfriend and gave birth unmarried, for instance, had to leave her apartment because it was reserved for childless couples. She recalls:

> I was on good terms with the landlady, so when the baby was born, I informed them that we had separated and that a child was born, but that I wanted to keep renting the apartment.... But I was told by the real estate agent that this was not acceptable, even if the landlady was fine with it, as it was an apartment where children were not permitted.

A change in marital status and family composition, therefore, could have direct repercussions for mothers' housing options, revealing the new conditions they came to face as single mothers.

Changes in mothers' financial circumstances, of course, could also be a reason for moving house. Hara Tomoko, for instance, was taking care of a preschooler and an infant when her husband suddenly left her for another woman. Dependent on payments from her husband, she was unable to work because her youngest was below one-year-old and she faced high rental payments for the family apartment. As a result, Hara decided to move to a smaller and cheaper apartment. The circumstances under which mothers came to look for housing alternatives, therefore, highlighted both the social and economic consequences of their new status and identity as single mothers.

But finding housing as a single mother was often a complicated affair. In the period following a sudden breakup or separation, many therefore sought temporary refuge with their parents. A small but significant minority of mothers also decided to move back with their parents at a later stage, often due to financial reasons and in order to be able to combine work and parenthood more easily. According to the national survey on single parent families, more than one third of divorced and unmarried mothers reside with their parents, grandparents, or siblings (MHLW 2011), which may be attributed to the various benefits of co-residence for single mothers' well-being (Raymo and Zhou 2012).

Yet, family support was not available to everyone and was more common among families with more stability in income and more resources (cf. Iwata 2001). Mothers who resided with their parents were mostly university-educated and had married parents who owned their family home and a father with a stable income. By contrast, mothers who grew up in low-income or single-parent families were less likely to be able to stay with their parents and to rely on their support. Kato Minako, for example, very briefly stayed with her family after she decided to divorce, as she had no income as the mother of an infant and her husband had gambled away their savings and burdened her with debts. However, she saw staying with her parents only as a temporary option. She explains: "My parents are ordinary people, but they are not very rich. Going back meant living in the same small place with them, with my adult brother, and that was not a comfortable place to go back to. So I decided I had to do things on my own. I was really starting from zero and from there, entered a shelter for single mothers."

In other cases, the regulations governing public housing units, which limit the permissible number of residents to registered family members, could prevent mothers from seeking family support. Yoshida Megumi, who urgently needed to find refuge from domestic violence, felt that she would cause trouble for her family if she stayed with them. Since her family lived in a public housing unit, returning even briefly could result in eviction for exceeding the official number of residents.

In searching for an apartment of their own, mothers also came to face prejudice and discrimination as single mothers. Toyohashi Mariko, a divorced high school graduate who separated when her son was an infant, reports: "When I looked for a room in [Tokyo], and said that I am a single mother, I was told [by the real estate agents], 'We don't have anything available.'" Even though few had had difficulties finding an apartment as working single women, the presence of small children made many real estate agents and landlords unwilling to consider them as tenants. But it was not necessarily just the presence of children, but also her marital status that apparently made Toyohashi an undesirable tenant. She further explains: "In the end, I lied to find a place [to live]. I was not officially divorced yet, so I could show them my family registration without any problems. So, instead of saying I was a single mother, I said my husband is working in another city [*tan'shin funin*]." The absence of a breadwinner, therefore, could be taken as an indicator of a lack of financial resources, as well as a potential "problem" family.

In addition to their marital status, mothers' incomes became an issue in finding rental housing. Self-employed women had little proof of a stable salary, while others held low-paying jobs or were in the process of looking for work, providing them little proof of financial viability. As Saka Hideko, a divorced mother of two high school students, puts it: "Someone like me, who is self-employed.... If I was working for a large company or were with the University of Tokyo [like the interviewer], I could rent a room, but if you are playing piano without being particularly famous and, in addition to that, are a single mother with children, it is hard to find a room."

Beyond status and job security, in many cases the ability to rent a room came down to a matter of cost. Matsui Shigeko explains:

> If I was living alone, an apartment would cost between ¥60,000 and ¥70,000, ¥75,000 [US$545—$682] a month at the most. The place where I lived before [giving birth] cost ¥70,000 [US$636]. So when I said [to the real estate agent] that this would be the price range I expected, he told me that for a mother and child there was no place at such a price. I was told it would at least cost ¥90,000 [US$818].... Because in regular [wooden-structure] apartment buildings one would hear the child crying, I had to look for a *mansion* [an apartment in a concrete building] where her voice could not be heard.... [But] with my income, I couldn't pay for that.... My new place costs ¥60,000 [US$545]; it's in a mansion, but probably about forty years old. A six-mat room [ten square meters], with a kitchen.... It is, of course, very old and worn, but since I did not have a place to live [I had no choice].... Below, there is actually a pub. Even if the baby cries, one can only hear the karaoke until about 2 a.m. It's not that one hears it all that much, but even if the child cries, it is not much of a problem. So, finally, I can peacefully live here.

The key issue was thus not merely the presence of children or income alone, but the fact that cheap Japanese-style apartments in wooden structures have very thin walls. Although apartments in concrete buildings do not have this problem, they usually come with considerably higher rents, unaffordable for a single mother with an average monthly income of ¥150,000 to ¥200,000 (US$1,364—$1,818). Here, too, therefore, resources played a role. While university graduates with a stable office job did not raise the rent on their apartment as a major issue, it could become a serious difficulty for those with low or unstable incomes.

If a mother received public assistance, moreover, the budget for renting an apartment was limited to ¥60,000 (US$545), further restricting her options, leaving aside the fact that the apartment would have to house a family. Sakai Yoshimi describes her search strategy:

> I went to about eight real estate agents. I told them straight away, "I am receiving public assistance, I have children, and I need a one-room apartment for no more than ¥60,000 [US$545]." They all looked at me with such pity! But they kindly explained to me all kinds of things. They said that if you go to real estate agents from big chains, you won't be offered anything, and that it is better to go to old real estate agents who have roots in the community. Rather

than those "on the hill" [i.e., in more affluent areas], it is better to go to lower city [*shitamachi*] real estate agents, who might be more likely to rent something to me. They pulled out a map, and said, "If you look around here, these here, they might rent to you." And I went there as I was told. But I had to go to about eight places. With the children in tow. It was tough.

While Sakai herself came from a low-income family, for others such a journey to the communities of the lower parts of the city could be symbolic of their downward mobility and socioeconomic displacement on having become a single mother.

The high prices for family housing could also mean that mothers ended up renting apartments they could barely afford. Yonekawa Sachiko explains:

> I looked for one year but could not find anything. I was turned down as a woman, a single mother, and an artist working in the entertainment industry.... In the end, I found a place nearby, which costs ¥160,000 [US$1,455 per month], a forbiddingly high price, but I had to register my son for school [for which a residential address was required]. We found the place only one week before school started. My landlords told me that paying such a high rent as a woman is a real achievement. They said: "Work hard [*gambatte kudasai*]!"

Single mothers' search for housing, therefore, challenged mothers not only to find housing with a limited budget, but also to make difficult choices and set priorities between their earning potential and income, housing conditions, and their children's needs.

Miura Natsu also took a big risk in renting a high-priced apartment out of desperation. After a brief return to her family in the countryside, she decided to move back to Tokyo, where work opportunities and social circumstances would be more favorable. This meant, however, that she would have to find an apartment in a very short period of time. As she recounts:

> I came to Tokyo during the Golden Week Holidays, stayed in a youth hostel, and looked for a place. As for the children, I somehow convinced my family [to take them in the meantime], because I had to look for housing. But, of course, in such a short time, I couldn't find anything. There were a lot of problems. The children, that I was going to bring them up by myself as a single mother, that was a big shock. But then I found this one place, which was quite expensive, ¥110,000 [US$1,000] a month. And I already knew that I would not earn much. So I lied, and told them that I was on leave from work, and that I received child support payments. That's how I was able to sign the rental contract. I went back to the company I had quit, and told them if someone called, they should just say I was on childcare leave [rather than out of work]. The boss of the company was also there, and luckily I was told I could have my old job back.

While Miura considered herself lucky to have been able to find work and housing, she also faced tremendous pressure and a tight budget in making ends meet due to the high rent of her apartment.

The possibility of entering low-cost subsidized public housing, therefore, constituted an attractive alternative, particularly for high school graduates with a low income and little savings. Nationwide, 18.6% of divorced and unmarried mothers live in public housing, offering a unique source of support to single mothers with low incomes (MHLW 2011). Kimura Eiko, for example, had been able to keep the public housing apartment she had rented during her marriage, offering her not only continuity and stability after separation, but also considerable financial relief because of the low rental cost of the apartment. As she says:

> I lived [in this public housing apartment during my marriage] and stayed here after I divorced. He was the one who left. That's why I didn't really think I had a hard time, as compared to others. Even those who have children of the same age and divorce, they have to pay a higher rent. But because I stayed in a public housing unit, it is different from a rented apartment. An apartment of this size [two rooms and a dining kitchen], in this area, that would cost about ¥150,000 [US$1,364] per month. That would be hard to pay. But if you live here and you are a single mother, it is almost free.

In light of the struggles described by others to rent an apartment with children, public housing units offered a safe space, stability, and considerable support for those with few financial means and resources.

Many mothers, therefore, applied for such an apartment in order to relieve themselves of the pressure of high rental costs for private apartments. Although there are long waiting lists, their status as single mothers can translate into priority treatment, increasing the chances of entering public housing sooner rather than later. Kato Minako describes her experience: "Everyone was applying for years but, somehow, soon after I got [to the shelter for single mothers], I got a place, while others didn't get in. It is a lottery and you get points. Nobody else got in, only me. I really felt bad. For two, it is pretty big. Five-and-a-half mats, six mats, three mats [rooms of five to ten square meters in size], it is 3K [three rooms and a kitchen]." Without such assistance, she is likely to have rented a single (fifteen square meter) room with a kitchen at considerably higher cost.

In this way, the search for a new residence on becoming a single mother not only marked a period of transition, but also confronted mothers with the social and economic dimensions of life as a single mother. As single mothers taking care of small children and with a low income and earning potential, their housing options became considerably narrower, marking their new position in Japanese society. Resources, of course, also mattered. In addition to personal income and savings, family support and public subsidies played a central role in their search for a new residence, generating different opportunities for single mothers from different social backgrounds. University graduates from families with a higher social standing often benefited from more family support, while public assistance and subsidized public housing offered a unique safety net for those with the least resources, means, and educational credentials. Those with neither family nor public support, therefore, faced the most difficult challenges, as they had to manage high housing expenses with their low incomes. This, of course, not only affected their housing situation, but also put pressure on them to maximize their income from work.

FINDING A JOB

One of the most characteristic aspects of single motherhood in Japan is that most single mothers work, despite the fact that a temporary break in employment and part-time employment remains the dominant trend among married mothers. This understanding that employment is considered the main source of single mothers' income is also evident in the employment trends of women who become single mothers. As the nationwide survey of families headed by single mothers indicates, 69.1% of mothers who had not been employed at the time of their separation had found employment by the time they were surveyed (MHLW 2011). Even if mothers were working at the time of separation, the prospect of having to manage work and childcare and to support the family on their own could mean that they approached employment in a new way. As compared to married mothers, the incidence of job change is considerably higher among single mothers and is motivated by the need to earn a higher income and find more suitable working conditions (JIL 2003, 153f).

The complex initial struggles particularly facing mothers who were not employed at the time of separation are illustrated by Hara Tomoko's story. Deserted by her husband shortly after the birth of her second child, she took whatever job she could find under the circumstances, which, however, only ended up pushing her to the very edge. As she describes her situation:

> [At the beginning] I could not do regular work. I was only able to work selling life insurance [as a door-to-door saleswoman] because I had a baby. I thought whatever earns me some money would be okay, although others advised me to look for a stable job soon. But, in the end, my children were in two different day care centers, which was really difficult in the mornings. I also paid for an expensive apartment and had no stable income [as it depended on the ability to sell life insurance].... I also learned that it would be better to finalize the divorce, to be able to get the dependent children's allowance, and leave aside the question of alimony.... Because he was in debt and because of the recession, I decided not to go to court and just demanded custody of the children, so

that I could finally get state support.... But, then, because of the recession, selling life insurance became difficult.... It became difficult to pay my rent.... By the end of the year, I was almost without income, lagging behind on my rent.... I was also visited by someone from the welfare office, because neighbors had told them that I was leaving the children on their own in the evening, when I went out to work. I was offered public assistance. I only had to sign to receive it, but I just could not do it. I am a university graduate, and my parents as well, and they also got through thick and thin even if times were difficult. I just could not bring myself to do it.

Hara's story portrays the multiple challenges faced by single mothers upon separation. As a mother taking care of children below school age, the availability and logistics of day care considerably limited her employment options. Door-to-door selling of life insurance is a typical initial job in such a situation and counts among the few occupations, besides hostessing, that openly welcome single mothers as employees. As Hara's experience shows, however, after the initial period of guaranteed income had passed, it became increasingly difficult to secure an adequate income despite her best efforts, as her salary came to depend on the number of newly secured contracts.

Hara's desperate situation also highlights her understanding that child support payments from her children's father were unlikely to become a major source of support for her livelihood. Worried that her financial circumstances and demands for child support payments could only jeopardize her ability to claim custody of her children, Hara made finalizing her divorce, even without a monetary settlement, a priority. Rather than insisting on her children's right to child support payments, she was eager to finalize her divorce so as to become eligible for state assistance in the form of the dependent children's allowance.

Despite her dire circumstances, furthermore, she resisted reliance on public assistance, highlighting the stigma and downward mobility associated with being on "welfare" and, in turn, the centrality of employment as the main source of single mothers' income. As a consequence, Hara tried to manage on an income below the level of what she would have received as recipient of public assistance, exposing herself and her children to extremely difficult living conditions. This is a common pattern: as the high percentage of single mothers living below the poverty line indicates (Abe 2008; Akaishi 2014), many choose to support themselves with a low income rather than rely on public assistance.

While single mothers' eagerness to lift themselves up by their bootstraps and support themselves through employment may appear admirable, it also poses the question of the actual conditions for becoming financially self-sufficient as a working single mother. What are the reasons mothers continue living on low incomes, despite their best efforts? And what factors and conditions could make it possible for single mothers to earn a family wage?

THE IDEAL-CASE SCENARIO

While the work-family balance was a challenge facing all single mothers, there were a few mothers who stood out because they earned a stable salary that was high enough to disqualify them for state assistance in the form of the dependent children's allowance. Ideal cases for any policymaker aiming to enforce single mothers' economic independence, they managed single motherhood even without special state allowances. Consider, for instance, Yoshioka Rie, a university-educated mother of a five-year-old. Employed as a public servant and public school teacher since her graduation from university, Yoshioka not only has a permanent position, but also an annual salary of ¥7.0 million (US$63,636), which by far exceeds the income limits for subsidies and allowances for single mothers. Yet, while she may be considered an ideal case, the particularities of her situation also highlight the role of the specific conditions and resources that made possible her financial independence and stable position.

Yoshioka grew up in a progressive middle-class family, with parents who encouraged her to seek employment and a career, at a time when a university education for women was still uncommon. While almost all of her female schoolmates desired to get married and become a "bride" (*oyomesan*), she was fascinated as a child with the idea of being a craftsman. When she entered university, her interests shifted to teaching and education and, after graduation, she found a job as a teacher in a public school. In her mid-twenties, Yoshioka married, but divorced a few years later.

Finding herself unexpectedly pregnant in her early forties, she came to face a situation with many challenges and uncertainties. She knew nobody else who had given birth outside of marriage and at her age. But her workplace turned out to be very accommodating of her needs. When she announced the news to the school management, they matter-of-factly responded that they would arrange for a maternity leave replacement. Yoshioka was able to take a year-long maternity leave, living on a small allowance and savings. When she returned to work, she was placed in a class with relatively few demands, where she could rely on other teachers whenever she had a childcare emergency. As she notes:

> Without the childcare and the maternity leave, I would not have been able to come this far.... Since I do not have relatives or family nearby, if there was not such support at my workplace, I would not have been able to make it.... I am grateful to those who helped me out then. In my case, everything went smoothly thanks to my colleagues.

Although she felt alone and hesitant to ask friends and family for help, Yoshioka was able to manage with the support of an accommodating workplace and basic public services. In preparation for her return to work, she applied early and obtained a place for her daughter in a day care center nearby her home. That way, she could drop off her daughter right after the opening of the day care center at 7:30 a.m. and still be on time for work at 8:10 a.m. Although her work often extended to evening hours, with phone calls from parents and class preparations, she could usually leave her workplace and take work home if necessary; and, although time was tight, she could usually pick up her daughter just in time before the day care center closed at 7 p.m. To manage emergencies, she registered with the local "family support service," which provides help with childcare through the local government. While her everyday life is hectic, she feels assured by the job security she enjoys as a public servant.

Yoshioka's case highlights the possibility of women's and single mothers' economic independence, but also needs to be recognized as a rather unique case. A university graduate, she obtained a qualification and permanent employment soon after graduation, and she kept her position without interruption throughout marriage and after she gave birth to her daughter. The fact that she was a seasoned teacher, with a permanent appointment, also provided her with considerable assurances and support at the time she gave birth. She had savings and a partially-paid maternity leave of one year, and she benefited from a family-friendly workplace after returning to work. Although her work hours are long, she is able to manage day care center hours because of the possibility of doing some of her work preparations at home.

One key factor that allowed some women to earn a considerably higher wage even as single mothers was continued employment in a full-time and, in some cases, career-track position. This applied more often to mothers who gave birth outside of marriage, who were less likely to have interrupted their employment in entering a relationship, and who had often worked themselves up to a relatively good salary by the time they had children. But some divorcees also had continued to work throughout their marriages. Yamamoto Akiko, for example, earned an even higher income than Yoshioka working full-time for a multinational company. But the presence of a child, and her status as a single mother, made her concerned about her future employment. Unlike Yoshioka, she did not enjoy the same assurances as a civil servant but felt pressured to keep up her performance and minimize the impact of having a child on her work performance.

Her concerns about her future were reflective of the risks facing women working in the private sector. Watanabe Takako, a university graduate and divorcee, for instance, worked in a full-time job initially, but fell into difficulties over the long run. Her job demanded long hours regardless of her daughter's age and made it considerably more difficult to take a day off to care for a sick child or, for that matter, to ask for understanding for her role and responsibility as a mother so as to avoid overtime work. Unlike Yoshioka, she did not benefit from the same employment security and family-friendly workplace and was demoted to a lower position with a significantly reduced salary when her daughter became a teenager, which made her for the first time eligible for the dependent children's allowance.

Where Yoshioka was able to rely on permanent employment as a civil servant, mothers employed in the private sector more often relied on family support in managing the work-family balance. Obuchi Miho's ability to work full-time and maintain a permanent position at middle age, for instance, clearly benefited from her co-residence with her mother, in addition to her qualifications as junior college graduate and clerical accountant. Giving birth unmarried in her late thirties, after the end of a childless marriage, she had held a job in a small company for a number of years. Not wishing to burden her colleagues with extra work, she worked up until the day of her child's birth and returned after six weeks of maternity leave, leaving her infant in the care of her mother. When her daughter became older, she entered day care. She recounts:

> In the morning, I would drop her off on the way to the station and go to work. The day care center closed at 19:00 so I could make it to pick her up [with an hour long commute]. [When she was ill,] I would ask my mother and, if my work schedule would allow it, I would take her to the hospital and have my mother look after her, and go to work late.

This was, however, only an option because she could rest assured that her mother would be able to help out if she had to work late and would not be able to make it to the day care center before closing time. The presence of her mother offered great reassurance and supported employment stability. Obuchi had no concerns about her work performance and her income exceeded the income limit for the dependent children's allowance. Indeed, research-based survey data indicates that single mothers who reside with their family actually tend to spend less time and have fewer meals with their children (Raymo, et al. 2014), meaning that co-residence supports single mothers' employment but can also lead to longer commutes and work hours and less time with children.

The significance of parental support in facilitating mothers' employment was most clearly highlighted by Takezawa Hideko's experience. A junior college graduate, she entered employment without a clear direction upon graduation, but settled into a career-track job at a large corporation at the age of twenty-three. As she continued working at the same company for twenty years, she advanced to a fairly handsome salary. Faced with an unplanned pregnancy in her late thirties, she was able to take an unpaid maternity leave by relying on savings and residence with her mother. Her mother's assistance also allowed her to manage her full-time job despite a ninety-minute commute. She relates:

> I found a public day care center and was able to shorten my work hours in the first year [after giving birth] to from 10:00 to 16:30, and later from 9:30 to 17:00, to allow me to spend a little more time with my daughter. But because of the commute, it was still hard to make it to the day care center during its open hours.

Eventually, the fact that she had to take off from work when her daughter was ill had repercussions on her work evaluation, leading to a lower bonus and lower salary increase. But she was still able to keep her job because of her mother's assistance. When her mother passed away, Takezawa tried to cover out of pocket extra day care after public day care center hours, but eventually collapsed and quit her job, being unable physically and financially to manage childcare and a full-time job. Not only was her twenty-year record at her company impaired by "low performance" due to childcare issues, her long work and commuting hours also became unmanageable without family support.

Central to mothers' ability to earn a high income, therefore, was not only uninterrupted employment and entry into a career-track position at a fairly early stage, but also job security in the form of a public sector job or family support, allowing them to manage the work-family balance more easily while maintaining a demanding job. Such cases are, however, more likely to be the exception rather than the rule.

M-SHAPED EMPLOYMENT

Whereas mothers who stayed employed without interruption faced the challenge of accommodating children's needs with their full-time job, the main initial problem for mothers who quit their jobs upon having children—a more common work pattern among married mothers—was to find employment that they could reconcile with parenthood. Their work trajectories not only highlight the challenges of managing the work-family balance but also the long-term implications of quitting the workforce upon marriage and childbirth.

To begin with, finding employment as a single mother was complicated by the need to take into consideration day care hours as well as childcare emergencies. As Yushima Kayoko, a junior college graduate and mother of two preschoolers, describes:

> When looking for work now as a [single] mother, the conditions are different from before [when I was single and childless]. Because of the day care center

hours, the need to go pick up the children [by 6:00 p.m.] and the need to take off [when the children fall ill]. That is the biggest difficulty, before income. And whether the employer will even take you if you will take more days off than other workers when the children get sick. If you can clear this up it's okay. Otherwise, you can't do it.

Because subsidized public day care centers close at 6 or 7 p.m., it is difficult to work at a full-time job that may require overtime work. As commuting times are considerable in a large city such as Tokyo, public day care center hours leave little to no space for overtime work. While this is a challenge faced by all working mothers, it makes reentry into the labor market for single mothers with small children all the more difficult.

As single mothers, employment was also not just a matter of earning an income, but also raised the question of their long-term income-earning prospects. Tokunaga Asami carefully considered her employment options shortly after separating from her husband:

> I wanted to become independent [from my parents' support] quickly, but it was just at the time when the so-called Bubble burst. I wondered what kind of work I should do. In any case, office work would be the first to be subject to cuts, so what should I do? I could wash dishes or do cleaning jobs, I didn't mind. But, then, thinking about having to raise a child, I thought I would need a certain level of income. If I don't have a stable income, I would have a problem. So I decided to go for professional training as a clerical accountant.

Tokunaga had been employed as a clerical worker before getting married, but without a long-term outlook on a career or possibilities for promotion. The fact that she had to support herself and her child meant that she had to look beyond occupations typically occupied by unmarried single women and consider obtaining specific qualifications that might ensure a job with greater earning potential and job security.

But even if mothers had qualifications and held career-track jobs, balancing children's needs with a full-time job could be very challenging. Kondo Naoko, who had worked as a graphic designer until her marriage, explained her decision to move into clerical work rather than continue in her career-track job as follows:

> Because of the day care center hours and because having personal time with my child is important to me, I wanted a job without overtime and with a regular income. I wanted a part-time job with an hourly wage and a monthly paycheck. Office work was best for that, but I had no relevant skills [e.g., in the use of Microsoft Word and Excel], so it was hard to find a job.

To acquire the necessary skills, she first worked part-time to acquaint herself with the basic use of word processing software used in clerical work and then searched for full-time employment, but with regular hours. She eventually landed a contractual office job much below her actual skills and earning potential, but with a reasonable hourly wage, predictable hours, and good benefits. The ability to work in a full-time, career-track position was, therefore, not just a matter of mothers' ambitions and qualifications. Because of the challenges of balancing work and family singlehandedly as a single mother, many considered part-time work as the most feasible option while their children were of preschool age, and planned to return to more demanding and higher-paying full-time positions once their children had reached school age.

However, even if mothers did their utmost to upgrade their skills and work toward a more stable position with a higher income once their children had reached school age, this expectation often proved hard to realize. Ueda Atsuko offers an illustration of the impact on her work trajectory of withdrawing from the workforce upon childbirth. A junior college graduate, Ueda worked as an accounting clerk in a small company after graduation. Having grown bored with the monotony of clerical work even after changing jobs a few times, she changed course in her mid-twenties, trying a job with more responsibility by becoming a manager of a small café. She says: "Until then I was an accounting clerk. I wanted to do some real job, something that would allow me to become independent." Obtaining this position increased her salary from about ¥2.0 to ¥4.0 million (US$18,182–$36,364) but it came with long workdays, from 7 a.m. to 8 p.m. Barely able to see the daylight because of her workplace's basement location, she quit after two years, realizing that even as a café manager she was only a hired employee, with no real independent decision-making power. Approaching her thirties, she felt disillusioned by the world of work and, anticipating marriage, decided to work as a temporary contract employee (*haken*) for about ¥2.8 million (US$25,455).

After she married at the age of twenty-nine, she continued working for a short while, but eventually quit after giving birth because of pressure from her husband. She stayed home with her daughter until her separation a few years later. In her early thirties, with a small child and no recent work history, she had difficulties finding work and settled for a part-time job. To upgrade her skills, she attended a six-month course at a vocational school, which helped her find a clerical job at a small company with an annual income of approximately ¥2.5 million (US$22,727). As she found it difficult to take off from work when her daughter fell ill, she used a home-help service provided by the local city government to cover for emergencies. In addition, she chose a job with a low workload and little responsibility, and worked hours of 9 a.m. to 5:30 p.m., which allowed her to pick up her daughter from the day care center by 6 p.m. While she had gained considerable work experience, the fragmented nature of her work history also led to limited earning opportunities in her thirties. Her annual salary had peaked at ¥4.0 million in her mid-twenties, dropping to ¥2.5 million (US$22,727) when she returned to clerical work after becoming a single mother.

Ueda's story reflects the changes and uncertainties facing women who anticipate marriage and motherhood rather than a career. Although Ueda had considerable work experience, she changed jobs several times and initially did not pursue professional qualifications or jobs with long-term outlooks. Because she had not worked for several years during her marriage and after giving birth, she found it difficult to reenter employment in her thirties. When she found a full-time job, however, her salary varied little from what she had earned in her early twenties.

Finding a stable job after a break in employment proved even more difficult for high school graduates. Kato Minako's story provides an illustrative case here. Kato attended professional school and worked as a hairdresser until her marriage. Although her initial salary was too low for her to be able to live independently, she gradually worked herself up to a salary of ¥2.8 million (US$25,455). Married at the age of twenty-seven, she quit hairdressing and, at her husband's family's request, worked part-time in the office of his parents' family business. Eager to add to the family income, she then took care of clerical work for the family company. When she divorced shortly after her daughter's birth, she felt pressured to find a job to support herself and her daughter as soon as possible. However, she was unable to get back into hairdressing because she had not worked in the field for several years and she had no other qualifications and a small child to take care of.

Eager to boost her earning potential, she then applied for a six-month course in accounting in order to improve her qualifications. She explains: "When I was looking for work then, I earned only ¥700 [US$6.36 an hour], because I had no qualifications. But in the case of clerical accounting offices, I saw advertisements for hourly wages as high as ¥1,500 [US$13.64]." In searching for a new job as an accounting clerk, she was cognizant of the time and costs of a long commute and decided to narrow her search to jobs within thirty minutes of commuting time so as to be able to accommodate her daughter's needs. Yet, she found it difficult to find a full-time job and eventually settled for a part-time job as an accounting clerk for ¥900 (US$8.18) an hour and an annual income of about ¥1.2 million (US$10,909).

Although this pushed her income below a taxable wage, having been able to enter a public housing unit Kato was able to make ends meet with the dependent children's allowance and income from work. Once her daughter entered elementary school, she searched for a full-time job and eventually found contractual employment as an accounting clerk with an annual salary of ¥2.8 million (US$25,455). She notes: "If you are over forty, it is hard to get an office job. Until thirty-five, there are jobs but now that I am forty-three, I think it is difficult. I am grateful and try not to complain. It would be great to find work elsewhere, but there may be none." Yet, although she had work for the moment, the future of her position remained uncertain, as she was dependent on the renewal of her annual contract.

Kato might be described as someone who has made significant efforts to find work by acquiring qualifications for jobs that promised a stable income, from hairdressing to accounting. In this respect, Kato stands out for her ability to improve her credentials and at least achieve full-time, though not permanent, employment. While her income is comparatively high for a high school graduate, it has, as in the case of Ueda, changed little since her twenties and is unlikely to increase in the future. Unlike mothers who remained continuously employed and pursued qualifications and a permanent position from an early age, mothers who quit work with marriage faced considerably narrower options and were unlikely to find permanent employment or reach an annual income above ¥3.0 million (US$27,273).

A notable exception to this pattern was found for those in public sector jobs, in particular in positions as kitchen personnel in schools and day care centers. Yushima Kayoko, who had returned to work after a break in employment when she separated, was fortunate to secure such a position. Working part-time to begin with, she soon realized the importance of looking for more long-term options. Thirty-nine years old, she considered public sector employment a unique option. She explains:

> There was a limit to working in a part-time job because of the basic labor law. I realized that I would not be able to continue working in the same job [after five years] and, since I was close to forty and I was told by others that at forty I could no longer get a full-time position, I started worrying about whether I would be able to find work until my child—who was born when I was thirty-six—came of age. I by coincidence saw application materials to become a public servant and I applied. I got through the first round in the first year, but was put on a waiting list. The following year, I missed the [civil service] exam because my daughter was ill ... but in the third year, I finally got accepted and got a job in the kitchen of a public day care center, from 8:30 to 5:15, standing all day. I was first paid about ¥120,000 [US$1,090] a month and, after a year, I also received the dependent children's allowance. It wasn't much but I was able to somehow make it. But now, I am paid based on seniority, so I receive about ¥300,000 [US$2,727] per month and lost the eligibility for the dependent children's allowance and all kinds of other benefits.... It's very exhausting work, but I got the job thinking about the future. While working, I always think, "Could life for single mothers raising children not be easier?".... But I am a permanent employee now. I have a secure future, even if I don't remarry and have to raise the children on my own.

Yushima was lucky to succeed in her search for employment in the public sector, but her experience also highlights the obstacles she had to overcome to be able to enter such a position. Even though Yushima had planned ahead in applying for the position, the unpredictability of taking care of small children meant that she was unable to take the exam on her first attempt, having few resources and no family support to rely on to take care of childcare emergencies. Her ability to find stable employment was, therefore, not just a matter of preparation and diligence, but also seemed to depend on her ability to manage the application process while taking care of small children.

Also others recognized the advantages public sector employment offered, particularly for mothers with a break in their employment history. Hara Tomoko explains:

> People working in school kitchens are either people who get the job right out of school or women who used to be professional housewives and, for lack of other skills, get this kind of job. Some people say that insurance and school kitchen jobs were originally established to support war widows ... but nowadays there are also other kinds of people getting these kinds of jobs and some people say it's unfair to give single mothers preference in getting the jobs. That's why exams were introduced ... and it is becoming more difficult to get such jobs.... My income is now ¥5.0 million [US$45,455 a year] before taxes, so I lost eligibility for the dependent children's allowance last year.... [If I hadn't have gotten this job], I would have gone to the job center and, since I have a university degree, it is not that difficult to get a part-time job, that is, if one is not dependent on getting a permanent job.... But because of the bursting of the Bubble, it is getting more and more difficult to get a full-time job these days.

Public sector jobs, in this way, offered a safe haven for mothers: a permanent job with a good wage and family-friendly work hours, regardless of their work history and educational background.

Beyond this particular employment niche, however, finding permanent employment with a discontinuous work history was very difficult. Although many mothers improved their employment opportunities by acquiring specific qualifications, such as in elder care, childcare, clerical accounting, or medical-office work, finding permanent employment was often difficult particularly once they had reached an age of thirty-five and above.

EDUCATIONAL CREDENTIALS

If mothers who acquired special qualifications to improve their chances of employment had difficulties finding a job at middle age, however, their chances still appeared considerably better than those of high school graduates without these credentials. As has been documented by recent research, with the onset of the Heisei recession, part-time and irregular work became more predominant among high school graduates, and also university graduates faced more difficulties in finding permanent employment (Brinton 2011; Genda 2005). The lack of opportunity to develop work experience in low-skill, part-time jobs has also been shown to decrease the chance for stable employment and advancement in the long-term, not only due to limited qualifications but also due to the type of employment experience gathered (Kariya 2010). Even with a continuous effort to make ends meet through employment, therefore, irregular employment in low-skill jobs can lead to an uncertain future. Stratification in employment, consequently, is no longer just a matter of gender differences, but also of unequal opportunities among women of different social backgrounds (Kurotani 2014; Tachibanaki 2008).

High school graduates who reached adulthood during or after the bursting of the Bubble economy had mostly started working in their teens; while their wages were low and few, if any, anticipated a career or promotion, they were conscious of the need to work in the long-term, not unlike part-time working women of working-class origins featured in studies of the 1980s (Kondo 1990; Roberts 1994). Kuroki Takemi was typical in this respect. Having started working odd jobs as a teenager, she took for granted that she would be working when she divorced at the age of twenty-four and faced the prospect of supporting herself and her three children, all under the age of six. As her own mother had always worked, she had no qualms about reentering employment after she divorced and managing on her own. The frequent absences of her own father had led to her growing up in a quasi-single-parent household and she seemed fearless about the prospect of becoming a single mother. As she recalls: "I thought I would first of all try to borrow some money from my sister, who has a good income. I thought I could maybe stay with her, and work day and night. I used to work in a [twenty-four-hour] family restaurant every other day until 5 a.m." Eventually, however, she managed to obtain public assistance, while continuing to work in a small shop labeling goods for a few hours a week at ¥750 an hour (US$6.82)—the minimum wage. Although she would have liked to work more hours, she was unable to extend the day care center hours for one of her children, because of his special needs. Yet, like others, she planned to get full-time work once her children were in school. She says: "I feel that once the children are in school, they will strongly encourage me to leave welfare. They call that 'support for independence.' Of course, I will work for my children, but I also know that once you are no longer on welfare, it's really hard to get back." While motivated and eager to make ends meet on her own, Kuroki was well aware of the limits of "independence" through work.

But although high school graduates had worked as single mothers just like university graduates, particularly those of the Bubble generation had worked mostly in part-time jobs with hourly wages. As a consequence, their employment did not lead to a higher wage or prospects for better positions. More often, their employment took the form of low-skill jobs with an hourly wage, leading to other low-skill jobs. Goto Asami illustrates such a trajectory. Goto grew up in a family with four children, supported by a father who worked in various jobs in transport and distribution and a mother who worked in elder care. Goto herself first started working while attending senior high school, working at a convenience store for ¥750 (US$6.82) an hour. She then worked at a noodle soup (*ramen*) restaurant for ¥750 (US$6.82) an hour and later at a pub (*izakaya*) for ¥950 (US$8.64) an hour. Promised a "real job" by a friend, and feeling discouraged by her experience at school, she dropped out to find full-time employment. The job, however, turned out to be a hoax, and she ended up working as a *freeter*—a young person in irregular employment—at a gasoline stand (¥1,000/US$9.10 an hour) and, later on, working nights at a pachinko (pinball machine) parlor (¥1,300/US$11.82 an hour). After the birth of her daughter, she worked briefly in elder care but was forced to enter a shelter (rather than return to her parents) and to rely on public assistance, due to domestic violence and the threat of stalking by her former partner. Although Goto has worked throughout her adulthood and her hourly wage has increased incrementally, her work experience is composed primarily of casual part-time jobs she found through friends and job-search magazines. While aware of the potential benefits of qualifications, she does not feel that she has the resources at this point to make this possible, as she is expected to reenter employment as soon as possible as a recipient of public assistance. However, continued work in low-skill jobs is likewise unlikely to lead to anything but other low-paid low-skill jobs.

But high school graduates not only lack credentials; they also seemed to have less access to other formal and informal resources to support their pursuit of employment. Yoshida Megumi, for example, stands out as someone who was well aware of the need to work to make ends meet, yet had little knowledge of how as a single mother to approach her employment in the long run. Having grown up herself in a household headed by a single mother, she started working when she entered high school as a cashier at a local supermarket. Suffering the loss of her mother before the age of twenty, Yoshida then had to manage the care of two children without any family support when she divorced at the age of twenty-one. To support herself, she tried various jobs but had mixed success. When she worked part-time as a waitress, she was laid off after she missed work because of a child's illness. She was then recommended to work selling life insurance but, although she had a fixed salary at first, this declined rapidly after the probationary period when she failed to secure sufficient contracts. Later on, she tried factory work and worked in elder care. As her employment remained unstable due to children's illnesses as well as to trouble on the work floor and with her supervisors, the main source of stability for her was residence in a public housing unit, which considerably lowered her housing expenses. In addition, she received support through public assistance, allowing her to maintain a certain level of household income, even if her employment and salary fluctuated. As her salary was deducted from the amount of public assistance she received, she could be certain of a specific amount of income, with public assistance added to her low salary. Reaching the age of forty, her employment stabilized as she obtained training and continued to work as a supermarket cashier for a longer period of time, even though without a permanent contract. After twenty years of employment, however, she is no further along a career path than when she was a teenager and first worked in the very same occupation as a part-timer.

Facing the working world as a single mother from the age of twenty, Yoshida's case highlights not only the potential role played by family in providing support with childcare issues and the importance of qualifications in securing employment at middle age, but also the significance of strategies and dispositions in shaping employment trajectories. Where some mothers, such as Kato Minako, were alerted from an early age by their parents about employment prospects and had both the resources and knowledge to pursue and acquire specific credentials and qualifications, Yoshida entered the working world without such preparation. Although she has always exerted her best effort, she did not give her own qualities or future employment much thought, leading to a fragmented work history in a range of sectors and occupations. She found most of her jobs through introductions or suggestions from friends or simply by calling up local stores when looking for work. In addition, she lacked fundamental knowledge about the main rules and regulations governing work relations. As a consequence, she was unaware of the differences between contractual work and permanent positions and, although she had remained employed as a sales agent for a number of years, failed to secure a more stable contract by the time she reached the age of forty. In other words, although she was dedicated to supporting herself and her children, and made her best effort, her lack of knowledge about employment benefits and the conditions for permanent employment further complicated her ability to secure stable employment. She not only faced narrow employment options as a high school graduate without specific qualifications; she also had limited knowledge about how to pursue a more stable position, making her prospects of a permanent position even more unlikely.

While all the women shared the challenges of finding housing and employment, and building new lives as single mothers, therefore, there were differences in their resources and trajectories as single mothers. Their stories of finding a place to live underscored the structural displacement women experience in becoming single mothers, as they are not only faced with the challenge of supporting themselves and their children with limited resources, but also come to face differentiation because of their status as single mothers. The ability to find suitable housing also depended on access to resources, in particular family support and publicly subsidized housing, the latter offering relief from having to search for an apartment on a very tight budget. In balancing work and family and earning a family wage, parental assistance with childcare and in childcare emergencies and family-friendly workplace policies also played a crucial role. However, it was continued and career-focused employment that seemed to make the most significant difference in securing stable and better-paid employment in the long term.

A central issue facing working single mothers is, therefore, not just the work-family balance but, more importantly, the impact of an interruption in employment and of gendered expectations that emphasize marriage and full-time motherhood as a major source of status and recognition on long-term work opportunities. Single mothers' employment trajectories were shaped not just by their qualifications, credentials, resources, and efforts, but also by the gender elements of their life course. Getting married in a timely fashion and quitting work upon having children in order to adjust to the needs and demands of family life not only contributed to a break in their work experiences, but also came with considerable costs, as these choices largely foreclosed the possibility of earning a family wage and maintaining a middle-class living standard as a single mother.

Chapter Five

Motherhood and Class

As we have seen, earning a family wage as a single mother is a major challenge, despite the fact that most mothers work full-time. A low income, moreover, not only constrains the household budget, but also has potential implications for a single mother's everyday living conditions and can make it difficult to maintain the living standard and lifestyle a mother may see as most appropriate for herself and her children. How mothers manage their tight budgets, however, cannot be explained purely by available material resources, but also must be related to specific expectations about living standards and family lifestyle. For instance, while high school graduates on average lived on a lower income, many seemed quite matter-of-fact and resilient about their living conditions. University-educated mothers who had achieved an affluent living standard during their marriage, in turn, more often expressed a sense of constraint and downward mobility in having to make ends meet on a single salary, despite having a relatively high income compared to other single mothers. Their interpretations of their living conditions as single mothers, therefore, were not just a reflection of their material circumstances, but were also informed by their dispositions and views about what constituted an appropriate living standard for themselves and their children.

Maintaining a desired living standard and lifestyle as a single mother, moreover, comes with contradictory demands, on the one hand, of ensuring as breadwinners their children's material well-being and, on the other, of providing care for their children. A mother may feel challenged to take a full-time job in order to provide an income that supports a middle-class living standard and a higher educational attainment, but may also want to stay at home to be able to care for her children while they are young, consistent with the professional housewife ideal. In a situation where reclaiming all aspects of the identity to which they aspired as a mother may be impossible, mothers are forced to renegotiate economic, social, and cultural aspects of their social identity, and invest strategically in those elements they consider most central for supporting their desired lifestyle for themselves and their children. Their practices and interpretations in coming to terms with their situation thus reveal both dispositions toward and understandings of motherhood, as well as struggles to assert or maintain their identity. In this sense, mothers' everyday practices—the setting of the "right" kind of priorities to ensure a child's future success—not only highlight class-specific dispositions toward motherhood, but also offer insight into strategies of maintaining children's social status through financial, cultural, or symbolic means.

In this chapter, I examine single mothers' living conditions after they become single mothers, exploring both their dispositions toward and interpretations of their living standard as well as their everyday strategies in coming to terms with their situation. In so doing, I map the class-specific meanings of motherhood and the reproductive strategies mothers deploy in coping with their social position as single mothers.

MANAGING THE HOUSEHOLD BUDGET

The implications of limited household finances for a family's lifestyle were most clearly visible in mothers' housing conditions. As we have seen in the previous chapter, finding affordable housing as a single mother was often challenging, leading many to reside in small, Japanese-style apartments. Ikegami Satoko was typical in that she rented a private one-room apartment in a small building in an old residential district in the center of Tokyo after becoming a single mother. Composed of a small kitchen corner at the entrance of the apartment, which doubled as the hall to both the bathroom and the "living room" with a six-mat (ten square meters) tatami-mat floor, the apartment was a tiny space for mother and daughter to occupy. When her daughter was a preschooler, the main room was furnished with a small television and a small foldable table the size of a coffee table, which was put away at night to roll out the futon mattresses they shared. As her daughter grew older, she added a narrow shelf with books and a small desk for school work, which made the room visibly more crowded. The lack of private space, according to Ikegami, led to conflicts, which to her embarrassment were frequently overheard by neighbors, due to the thin wooden structure of the building, typical of Japanese-style apartments.

Subsidized public housing apartments offered a considerably more spacious alternative. Kato Minako was lucky to reside in such an apartment in a residential district on the outskirts of Tokyo. In contrast to the bare concrete staircases of the five-story housing complex without an elevator, her apartment felt like a warm and colorfully cluttered escape. With an open kitchen with a linoleum floor facing the entrance, the main living space was constituted by two small tatami rooms and one regular-sized one that were partially separated by sliding doors. The walls of the rooms were lined with small shelves and plastic containers, and a desk with her teenage daughter's books and study materials. As Kato had little income and was struggling to extend her temporary contract, the apartment offered her a sense of stability and comfort despite her economically precarious circumstances.

But although Kato felt reassured by the stability and comfort afforded by her residence in the public housing apartment, the class dimensions of living in a public housing apartment did not escape her daughter, who was about to enter middle school at the time of our interview. Comparing her own home to that of others, her daughter took issue at the lack of privacy and space. Kato explains: "She says she would like to live in a house [as opposed to an apartment]. She has said this for a long time. But I say this is impossible for me. So I say: 'Find a husband who can buy you a house.'" From her daughter's perspective, their lifestyle stood in great contrast to the middle-class suburban family homes she saw on television. Even Kato's own interpretation, in suggesting her daughter should find the right kind of husband who could afford to buy a house, underscored the benefits afforded by a middle-class marriage and a male breadwinner in the family. Although residence in a public housing unit offered considerable economic benefits, it also symbolized the socioeconomic repercussions of becoming a single mother.

The limits of mothers' budgets were also noticeable in the often very simple interiors of their homes and in the reception single mothers offered me when I visited for an interview. Kuroki Takemi, a high school graduate and mother of three children who lived in a private, two-room apartment and who received public assistance, for instance, apologized for not being able to serve coffee when I visited her at her home, stating that she had no milk for coffee in the house. It later turned out, however, that she did not drink coffee and never bought coffee to begin with. She sighed in relief when she realized that I was happy with a glass of cold barley tea (*mugicha*)—a typical children's drink on a hot summer afternoon—instead of coffee. Several other mothers, some of them working, though on part-time or short-term contracts, also appeared not to have green tea or coffee in the home. Instead, they offered me, as their guest, ready-made bottled green tea or iced coffee, which they had bought just for the occasion.

While it was not necessarily a matter of putting food on the table, mothers with a low or unstable income were also clearly more conscious about the need to use their limited funds strategically. Some mothers reported temporarily stopping their newspaper subscriptions when they became single mothers and economizing on the use of an air conditioner in the summer or using, as a rule, hand-me-down children's clothing. When asked about how they made sure they could make ends meet on their household budget, a number of mothers also confidently shared their strategies of making do with very little. Kuroki Takemi, for example, explains: "Well, you just have to manage your budget well. I am quite particular about where I go shopping. I usually go to small neighborhood stores, where I just buy what I need. If you go to supermarkets, you are tempted to buy more, because they have discounts. Some things I buy in bulk in special shops, because it is cheaper." Kuroki was very savvy in managing her budget, having lived on a low income already during her marriage. Supporting herself with public assistance, therefore, seemed more of a question of practicality and an extension of her habitus.

Higuchi Keiko, a high school graduate who also received public assistance, similarly felt confident about managing with a very small household budget. As she described:

> When I was still married, I had a [monthly] budget of ¥20,000 [US$182] for food and household expenses, but I usually spent only ¥15,000 [US$136] and saved ¥5,000 [US$45]. I look at the advertising pamphlets and buy cheap things in different stores, and I only take the money for those specific items with me, so that I am not tempted to buy more.

Like Kuroki, Higuchi seemed to manage her budget with practiced routine. Although she spent little on food, this did not mean she was not able to cook a variety of meals. She remarked: "Something like cabbage [is a great vegetable to buy]—it's cheap, and you can cook all kinds of dishes with it." Rather than worrying about what sort of food she and her children would eat, Higuchi seemed to be more focused on the fact that she actually managed to make dinner despite her limited resources.

But thrift also had its limits, as Kuroki understood:

> In the end, there is the question as to how much you can bear. I am, for instance, the kind of person who just really needs fruits. And I can't bear hard toilet paper.... There is a limit to which you can be self-disciplined. I always save ¥1,000 to ¥2,000 [US$9—$18] to buy things I like.... So, I think I am doing pretty well—it really depends on how you define luxury and your standard of living.

While other parents might consider eating fruits a healthy choice, and the choice of softer toilet paper hardly a luxury, Kuroki could take neither for granted as a simple lifestyle choice in light of her tight household budget. Managing on a tight household budget was, therefore, not just a matter of managing to make ends meet, but also of making strategic lifestyle choices, in accordance with one's own expectations of what constituted an adequate lifestyle.

The disparities between their lifestyles and those of two-parent families became even more apparent as their children grew older and began to voice their unhappiness about being unable to keep up with the casual consumption and fashions of their peers. Managing to make ends meet on a limited budget, therefore, was no longer a matter of mothers' shopping or cooking strategies. Instead, their children's ability to keep up with the fashion and consumption habits of their peers became a space of struggle over the meaning and significance of their financial circumstances and social status. Ueda Atsuko offers her impressions:

> My daughter is now in middle school, and you wonder, "Why would public school cost so much money?" It's because everyone sends their children to cram school, in order not to fall behind at school. My daughter also goes to cram school.... Everyone goes, that's why she wanted to go.... She does not like her grades to fall. Everyone is like that. She also wants to have things. She is at an age when she thinks a lot about what other children think about her. She wants to wear something fashionable, but that costs money.... You feel forced to buy those things for her. It also costs a lot to send her to cram school. I always wonder why all these things cost so much. It's not as bad when they are young.... They want a mobile phone, which costs money. Already from the last years of elementary school, they want to be fashionable, they have fashion magazines.... During the summer vacation, the days are very long. She goes to a club and to cram school, so she has things to do, but she also has days off, so she goes to the shopping center to buy this and that, and I always ask myself whether all children spend that much money. I wonder whether she really has to buy a bottle of soft drinks every day—it costs several hundred yen per day. How much do you think that costs per month? As a parent, that's what you end up saying. So I say she should take a water bottle, but she says nobody uses such a thing. So I give her the money [for the drinks] just during the vacation, this is how I negotiate with her.... They also go bowling, and do this and that, which costs money. But if you don't let them go, they will be ostracized by their group of friends.... And from now on, she will want specific brand items. Once they want to have these things, they will find out that their parents can't afford it, and if you say they should get a part-time job, well, you can say that to boys but not girls. There are too many shady jobs [for girls] around....

Ueda's observations highlight the challenges her low income came to pose in her relationship with her daughter. While eager to provide her with a happy upbringing, the costs of urban teenage consumption and peer pressure came increasingly to highlight the disparities between their and other families' living standards and disposable income, disparities she feared could also affect the perception and treatment of her daughter among her peers. While peer pressure to conform to social standards is an issue faced by most teenagers, the inability to keep up with consumption and fashion further underlined for single mothers and their children the class dimensions of their lifestyle.

Educational expenses also posed a central concern. Kato Minako, aware of the fact that entering senior high school would incur additional costs, started planning ahead, therefore, before her daughter's graduation from elementary school. As her salary did not increase but she expected additional costs, she mainly cut down on non-essential expenses. She says:

> We might say, "Let's no longer use the PC [personal computer] and Internet [to be able to save more money]." We have an old Windows 98 [operating system], we could do without Internet, cable TV, J-Com. We watch it, but we could cut down there. We could do with less. I am wearing things from ten years ago; I scold her that she costs so much money. But because she grows, you need to buy new things. In the case of a child, you can't do anything about that. Because she is still in elementary school, she wears regular clothes, t-shirts. Next year, it will be uniforms. I heard that it costs ¥100,000 [US$909]. I saved it, so I don't have to worry. I heard that from other mothers. It's obvious that it will cost money. So, I am prepared.... [But] cram school also costs money. They all go [to cram school] these days. She says she does not want to go. She is only doing calligraphy, she quit *soroban* [abacus] lessons. And she does volleyball for ¥500 [US$4.55] a month. When everyone else goes [to cram school] in middle school, she will probably also go, but I think cram school might cost quite a bit.

While Kato was able to save for school uniforms and considered cutting some less essential expenses, cram school costs of ¥20,000 (US$182) a month or more (MEXT 2008) seemed hard to afford. Yet, Kato was well aware of the importance of a higher educational attainment for her daughter's future employment prospects. She relates:

> Thinking about the future, I think finding a job will become more difficult [for my daughter].... I hear there are many freeters [who work in part-time jobs in the long-term].... I think I may also need to think about the possibility of sending her to private [senior high] school, so we have talked about saving, we have talked about it together. So we say, "We don't waste money."... If she can go [to a university], that's great, but under current conditions, it does not look like it. But, actually, I would like her to be able to put it on her résumé, Japan is a credential society [*gakureki shakai*]. Even now, there is a big difference between graduating from high school and from university, when you look for a job. Where I work right now, they only take university graduates. I am a contractual employee, because I graduated from high school and went to a hairdressing school. If I look around, I see that they only take university graduates [at my workplace]. I realized this is how high school graduates get left behind. I am myself faced with this reality.

Kato, who worked continuously throughout her adulthood only to be faced by short-term contracts and unstable employment in middle age, was painfully aware of the declining significance of a high school degree and the growing difficulties facing high school graduates in finding permanent employment. For Kato, the ability to afford a higher educational attainment for her daughter was, therefore, not about prestige, status, or credentials, but about improving her daughter's chances of securing a minimum of financial stability and job security.

Adding to concerns about financing cram school, some mothers also recognized that supporting their children's chances of doing well in school was not necessarily just a matter of being able to cover the financial costs. Ueda Atsuko, who had many middle-class professionals among her circle of friends, became painfully aware of the role and importance of specific knowledge and selection skills, that is, of cultural capital, in determining a child's educational future. She explains:

> When I look at the children of my friends, who are the kind of people that have the chance to meet people and take advantage of opportunities, I see how they are able to make sure they get a good education. So, I also thought I would send my daughter to cram school if I can, that it would be better for her. I try the impossible [financially] by sending her to cram school. But I don't know what she will come away with and what the differences in life chances among people are really about. We talked about it.... [My friends] have information as to which [cram schools] have the good teachers, not just some university student working part-time. They say it's better not to send your children to such places. They send them to good schools. These are the things that are not visible to our generation. I had the chance to talk to the kind of people who get into the newspapers. They all studied hard, and they think they worked hard. But the difference is that when looking for a job and going to university, and managing a two-income home, they think about things.... They select the companies where they work and their husbands. They talk about the university to choose, and what jobs to pursue. It's not just about getting an education. They also think about how to educate their children. Not just cram school, but *which* cram school is good. They don't think about *whether* they get into the schools, they select the school that fits their child. They think about what *kind* of education is good.... I wouldn't have thought of that without talking to them.

Ueda was not only aware of the privileged access others had to "good schools" due to their higher incomes but, even more crucially, she recognized the centrality for middle-class children's futures of specific knowledge about schools and education and of the ability to make the "right" kinds of choices—in other words, of the possession of a certain cultural capital—in the selection of schools, employment, and even partners in marriage. Despite having obtained a junior college degree, she acutely felt that not only her own lack of financial resources, but also her limited cultural capital, would make it difficult to foster her daughter's educational advancement, despite her best intentions.

Mothers' stories, in this way, not only highlight the challenges of making ends meet on a low income and the need to manage the household budget strategically, but also underscore the socioeconomic repercussions of the living conditions of single mothers on their lifestyle and their children's future. Their strategies of coming to terms with their situation did not just constitute practical solutions for living with a limited income, but also reflected an awareness of the class dimensions of their lifestyle and the importance of material resources, cultural capital, and specific everyday practices in facilitating their children's future educational and employment opportunities.

THE WORK-FAMILY BALANCE

Yet, even though mothers were aware of the need to strive for a higher income in order to support a certain level of education, their ability to invest in employment and advancement was, in most cases, heavily dependent on their resources. To uphold a full-time career-track job meant long work hours, and only a few were able to afford private childcare services that could accommodate overtime work.

Consider, for example, the childcare arrangements of Watanabe Takako. Watanabe was among a small number of university-educated mothers in career-track jobs and was unique in managing the work-family balance without assistance or support from her husband or family. To accommodate her long work hours, she depended on a complex network of private services at considerable cost. Before her daughter was born, she already had made arrangements with a day care center. As she reports, "I looked for a place with twenty-four-hour opening hours. My work schedule was basically 8 a.m. until ... was it 8 p.m.? And because, naturally, I would not be able to finish on time, I would go to pick her up at 9 p.m., 10 or 11 p.m." After her daughter entered elementary school, Watanabe continued to rely on private day care services. She continues: "My daughter would go to the after-school club and from there again to the day care center. Babysitting does come at a cost, but one can rely on it and feel at peace." She had considered using the so-called home-help system, a public service organized on the municipal level, where volunteers help out with childcare or household needs on an incidental basis. But staffed by volunteers, that system, she felt, did not provide the necessary predictability and certainty. As a consequence, she depended heavily on private services, which came at a high cost, the latter of which, in turn, made it a prerogative for her to maintain a high performance and salary through continued employment.

The possibility of her daughter falling ill posed another problem. Here, too, private services played an important role. She describes her situation:

> Also, when it came to taking care of a sick child, you can take care of that with money. If she had a fever in the morning and I could not go to work, that would be a problem. Therefore, I looked for a doctor nearby that was open at 8 a.m.... At 8 a.m., he would look at her and offer his diagnosis and prescribe the medication. Then, I would bring her to the twenty-four-hour day care center, and if she would still need to go to the hospital, they would take her. If I was worried, I would come back to look after her after finishing basic tasks at work.

She sums up her experience of child-rearing: "I cannot say that I raised my child myself—I fixed it all with money." Watanabe's success in keeping a full-time job and pursuing her career, therefore, also came with considerable financial costs, and had the consequence of leaving little to no time for and control over her role as a parent.

But while Watanabe was able to balance work and family by relying heavily on private services, most mothers found access to private services out of reach, as the costs by far exceeded their budgets. As a consequence, most mothers, even if holding full-time jobs, had to manage the work-family balance with different strategies. To begin with, many looked for jobs with fixed work hours and without an expectation of overtime work, as well as with a short commute. To manage childcare emergencies, they relied on the few rights and benefits they had in their workplace: paid holidays. Tokunaga Asami, a high school graduate who worked at a small company as a clerical worker, relates:

> Since I work for a small company, if I take off because of illness beyond my paid vacation days, my absence will be taken off from my basic wage.... I still have some paid vacation, so I don't have a problem right now. I treat my vacation days with care, so if my child has a fever and I can't bring her to the day care center, I can make use of them. Even if I have a low fever myself, or if I would actually like to go out, I am too afraid to take a vacation [day]. Last year, I got mumps from my daughter. But I had no fever, so I continued working, even though I had a swollen face.... My colleagues tell me not to work too hard, but if I don't take my job seriously, I fear I may lose my job one day.

The pressures of work performance meant not only that mothers feared to take off if they themselves felt unwell, but also that they found it difficult to leave work when a child fell ill. Hara Tomoko felt that she had to give her job priority over the care of her children when she faced great financial difficulties shortly after her husband left her:

> If I get a call [from the day care center] because my child becomes ill, it is expected that I will soon come to pick them up. But if I am in an important meeting, which does happen, then I can be quite late in picking them up. I was often scolded for that. So, then, because it was starting to really bother me, and

> my older child entered school, I would sometimes have him take off from school and look after the smaller one in the summer.... Because of a feeling of competition and need, children become the victims.

Unable to pay for extra services or to rely on parents and weary of criticism from the day care center, she felt pushed to leave her children to take care of themselves because of the pressure to work and to maintain her income. Pursuing full-time work as a single mother, therefore, often left little to no time to provide the kind of care mothers considered appropriate for their small children. Dependent on their wages, mothers acutely felt the impact on their employment status and income of absences from work due to children's illness. Sakamoto Mitsue explains:

> The difference between single mothers and other working mothers is that one has a different sense of stability. When your child gets ill, there is the possibility that your income will decline [because of your absence from work]. If you have a husband, you can feel secure. But for single mothers, such things [as children's illnesses] soon influence everyday conditions.

Even if mothers felt secure in their job, they were aware of the potential long-term impact of absences and lateness on their performance and income. Kumagai Mikako notes:

> A child's illness can be a reason for losing your job—that's something I heard at the day care center. At this point, I can take days off when my children are ill, and there is some real understanding at my company. So I don't really have to worry about keeping my job. On the other hand, when you get evaluated, even when women are older, they end up in a lower salary scale. Because they are late or miss work, something that happens because of children's illness.

Mothers not only felt vulnerable to the impact of children's needs on their work performance; they also were aware of the relative lack of employment security and the implications of that for their long-term future. As Tokunaga Akemi stated, "Because I work in a small company, I always worry how things will work out, whether they will let me work until I am fifty or sixty. It's not the kind of work that only I could do. But if I have to leave my job, I also lose my place to live [in subsidized company housing]." As she did clerical work at a small company, she felt that she had no special skills and could easily be replaced by younger and lower-paid high school graduates, a trend that has also been observed in earlier studies (Ogasawara 1998). Her major concern was not just to keep her job, and balance work and family life, but also to avoid becoming a burden in old age for her daughter. Mothers' struggles to balance work and family were thus not simply a matter of maintaining their current income, but were also clearly informed by more existential concerns about their ability to stay employed and their children's long-term future, which many had to manage with very few resources.

MOTHERHOOD, CLASS, AND REPRODUCTIVE PRACTICES

But although mothers shared similar problems in managing their income and balancing work and motherhood, there were also differences in their dispositions toward and understanding of their children's options and possible futures. If the dominant ideal of motherhood expects middle-class mothers to be homebound "professional housewives" who dedicate much quality time to their children's upbringing, one of the main challenges facing university-educated mothers anticipating a middle-class living standard for themselves and their children in particular was to balance the need for income from work with their ambitions and priorities as mothers. On the one hand, the demands of motherhood often make it difficult for university graduates to consider full-time work after becoming parents (Ehara 2000; Nemoto 2008). As Kanbara (2000a) has shown, among university-educated couples with white-collar husbands, the women have a stronger tendency to stay at home and tend to emphasize the importance of parenting over work. On the other hand, university-educated parents tend to make significantly larger financial investments in their children's education, meaning that university-educated single mothers face considerable pressures to earn the necessary income to facilitate a middle-class living standard and education for their children, making income from work a high priority.

Among blue-collar couples, meanwhile, women rarely become full-time housewives and tend not to be as concerned with children's schoolwork. Moreover, as Kondo has argued, working-class mothers' employment could also be seen as an expression of their dedication to their families and children's welfare (Kondo 1990), allowing mothers to justify their absence from the home as being in the interest of their children's well-being. Working single-motherhood may, therefore, be experienced quite differently depending on a woman's social background and disposition.

Among my interviewees, two groups of women, at the opposite extremes of educational attainment, particularly stood out. Contrary to the observation that working-class women have a stronger tendency to work as mothers, it was a small number of women with bachelor's and master's degrees and the largest amount of resources at their disposal who had a stronger tendency to invest more time and resources in their work performance, contradicting the idea that stay-at-home motherhood is central to middle-class motherhood. Conversely, it was a small group of women with junior or senior high school degrees and from low-income family backgrounds who were among the few who worked at most part-time and who consciously prioritized time with their children as opposed to a full-time job.

Similar trends have been observed by research based on nation-wide survey data. As Chisa Fujiwara (2005b) has shown, single mothers' work participation rate varies significantly by educational attainment. Although university graduates are more likely to be full-time housewives than junior high school graduates (37.6% as opposed to 31.0%) when married, the reverse is true when becoming single mothers. Single mothers who are university graduates have a work participation rate as high as 94.4%, while single mothers with a junior or senior high school degree have a significantly lower work participation rate (76.5% and 87.1% respectively). That is, although high school graduates work to a greater degree than university graduates when married, it is university graduates, who have more resources and in some cases less recent work experience, who have a much stronger tendency to work and work full-time when becoming single mothers.

To explore more concretely the meanings of such seemingly contradictory tendencies in single mothers' work patterns and mothering practices, let us look in greater detail at the life stories of three single mothers of different class origins and levels of educational attainment. Their experiences and perspectives are not necessarily representative of all women of the same class background, as the boundaries are, in any case, porous, but rather to shed light on contrasting dispositions and practices of women at the outer extremes of the class spectrum, highlighting the potential relevance of economic, social, and cultural capital in their approach to parenting as single mothers.

Let me begin with the story of Tanaka Miyuki, which illustrates the experiences and perspectives of a woman from a comparatively privileged background. Tanaka received an elite private school education and benefited considerably from financial and informal support from her family as a single mother. As she was familiar with the living standards and norms associated with an elite education, her story illustrates the potential social and economic consequences of becoming a single mother for a woman from an upper middle-class background.

Tanaka's life story contains many of the characteristics of the idealized life course of a middle-class woman of her generation. Tanaka grew up in a well-to-do family in Tokyo, attended a prestigious private high school and university, married a successful businessman after graduation and became a full-time housewife. Her lifestyle however radically changed when she decided to divorce after several years of an unhappy and childless marriage. Pursuing her long-term aspiration, she obtained a master's degree with the support now of her parents and began to work part-time as a teacher. Moreover, fulfilling her dream of family and motherhood, she became pregnant and gave birth outside of marriage. As the mother of a small child, she shared many of the problems facing other single mothers. When I first met her, she was juggling two high school teaching jobs with one-year contracts and everyday life with a child below the age of six.

Unlike other mothers, however, she had contacts and qualifications, which made it easier for her to find a job. She also received considerable support from her parents, which made it possible for her to manage her everyday life with a small child and a low income. Tanaka was also among the very few who owned an apartment—a Western-style, two-bedroom apartment in a modern building in the center of Tokyo, which she had purchased with the help of her father after becoming a single mother. Her mother also regularly took care of her daughter when needed: if her daughter had a fever in the morning, Tanaka would call her mother, who would travel for one hour to arrive at her apartment shortly before Tanaka's departure for work. Without such arrangements, she explained, she would have difficulties keeping her jobs, as absences and lateness would make it difficult to get her contracts renewed.

Although Tanaka's everyday life was a delicate balancing act between work and her daughter's needs, her family's support and her cultural capital and social connections allowed her to manage and to afford living with a low-income and contractual employment. She knew that obtaining a long-term job after age forty would be difficult, yet she decided that it would be better to have more time with her daughter while she was small, even if it meant a lower personal income. As she states:

> My relatives tell me that it would be better for me to get a stable job, given my age.... But I think I want to get a stable job only once [my child] is a little older. In many schools, the working hours [for full-time teachers] are really long, even though the pay is good and there is security.... Right now, I have more time [for my child] and, although I have only a low income, I would like to continue like this for a couple of years.

Although she was eager to work and pursue a career as a teacher, she could not quite detach herself from the idea that it was best to spend more time with her daughter when she was below school age. As a teacher, she had more flexible work hours, but with two part-time teaching jobs she actually had as little leisure time as full-time working mothers.

Tanaka had much greater resources from which to draw than most other mothers, yet she also felt more strongly the implications of single motherhood for her social identity as a woman from an upper middle-class family. Having moved to her apartment after becoming a single mother and without adequate time and resources to invest in the interior design suitable for a middle-class home on her part-time salary, she felt uncomfortable about the fact that she wasn't able to offer me the kind of reception she thought would have been appropriate in a middle-class home. When we sat down for an interview at her dining table, she offered me green tea, apologizing for the fact that the Japanese-style teacups did not match the size and style of the coasters and that the Japanese sweets she offered were from a school event of the previous day. Later on in the interview, she offered me black tea with golden Hello Kitty spoons in Western-style gold-rimmed teacups with saucers. Tanaka thereby attempted to conform to the typical middle-class etiquette of serving black tea in Western-style cups with golden tea spoons, or green tea cups with coasters, but was well aware that her home lacked the full "equipment" and thereby diverged from the expected style befitting her social standing.

Supporting herself on a part-time salary also meant that she needed to keep food expenses low. Nevertheless, the lack of time appeared to be more central to her shopping and cooking strategies than expense. Although she would have preferred serving her daughter home-cooked food, she noted that she simply did not have the time and energy to do so, given her long work hours, and often purchased ready-made food items for dinner. For Tanaka, the problem, therefore, was not about putting food on the table per se. Instead, she felt constrained by the fact that, unlike a full-time housewife, she was unable to provide well-balanced and home-cooked dinners for her daughter.

Fearing discrimination, she also hid her identity as a single mother at work, claiming that her partner was working in another city (*tan'shin funin*). Employees of larger companies in Japan are quite regularly placed in branch offices in other cities and even countries, to such an extent that a father's absence can be relatively easily explained away. She further reported that among her peers—former classmates from high school—divorce and single motherhood were associated with a decline of status and concerns over children's education. At an alumni meeting of her former high school classmates, she overheard her classmates, many of them housewives and married to well-to-do businessmen, making disapproving comments about the upbringing of children who attend day care centers. She says: "Many still believe that it is best for children to be raised by their mothers until age three, and say such things as 'Because they are raised in a day care center, [they don't have manners],' but, when learning that my child goes to one, they quickly add, 'Oh, she is very well-behaved!'"

In addition, many seemed to fear that single motherhood would obstruct the ability to maintain children's class status. "Since I graduated from a school where a lot of children of good families go," Tanaka explains, "I heard that many worry that children of one-parent families cannot get into certain schools or jobs because of prejudice. I am not sure whether that is true, but that is an incentive for them not to divorce until their children are in those schools. There are a lot of families like that." What is at stake here, then, is not merely the norms of motherhood but also the ability to maintain the identity of a middle-class mother by ensuring children's educational success and stereotypical career at a large corporation.

Tanaka herself did not elaborate on her feelings about her own daughter's future but, in making these observations, she underlined the challenges she and her daughter faced. When I met her again five years later, her daughter was attending a public elementary school and a cram school and was approaching an age when many middle-class parents begin to think about high school entry exams and their children's educational future. While Tanaka was evasive about possible financial and social constraints on her daughter's education, she expressed the view that her daughter should pursue "her own interests" rather than a prescribed career. Even though attending the same private school and university as Tanaka herself did was common among children of her former high school classmates, she argued that doing so was not as important to her, as other schools are able to provide an education of "similar standards." Rather than conceding the possibility of more constrained educational opportunities open to her daughter, she stressed the importance of respecting her daughter's individuality as an alternative approach to a good education.

Tanaka's life trajectory visualizes the implications of becoming a single mother for a woman who lived the lifestyle of a woman from a well-to-do middle-class background. Becoming a single mother radically changed her everyday life and made her conscious of the repercussions of becoming a single mother for her identity as a middle-class woman as well as for her daughter's future. Whereas she had previously been able to take access to an exclusive education for her daughter for granted, as a single mother she was confronted with the possibility of prejudices facing her daughter as the child from a single mother household. Financial concerns, in Tanaka's case, were not central to her concerns; instead, her story highlights the perceived significance of her lifestyle and identity as a single mother for her daughter's upbringing and future opportunities.

Where Tanaka was particularly concerned about the social consequences of her identity as a single mother for her daughter's upbringing, Yamamoto Akiko worried most about her employment and income and the financing of her son's education. Raised in a family that ran a small but quite successful family business, she attended an academically ambitious high school but did not proceed to university. Only after several years of working at a large company, did she decide to obtain a bachelor's and master's degree, both of which she financed from her savings, so as to be able to further her career.

Her lifestyle after marriage had the features of a well-to-do dual-earner middle-class couple, and she and her husband resided in a luxurious three-bedroom apartment in a high-rise building in central Tokyo that was located close to the train station and to work. During her marriage, she outsourced many household and childcare tasks. Most often, she reported, it was her husband who brought her son to the day care center and took off from work whenever her son caught a fever. Moreover, "if I do the housework," she argued, "that means that my time is being sacrificed [for household chores]. To take advantage of my time this way also means taking advantage of me economically [in the form of unpaid labor]." To ease the tensions surrounding housework, she hired help for household chores and paid a tailor to make many of the handmade items required by day care centers, such as a bag for pajamas and aprons made of towels. Rejecting the idea of housework and childcare as a woman's task, she was more eager to obtain and maintain a well-paying career-track job.

But whereas Tanaka had been able to take her education and living standard for granted, Yamamoto saw her lifestyle as a middle-class professional as an achievement based on her own efforts. Her life trajectory was built on the ideal of meritocracy and the upward mobility promised by the postwar educational system. Proud of her achievements, she was particularly cognizant of the potential material repercussions of becoming a single mother. Food, she remarked, did not cost as much now, since her husband's penchant for more expensive foods, such as sushi, no longer figured in the grocery bill. Instead, medical expenses, babysitting costs, and long-term housing and education expenses were more central concerns. She notes: "In financial terms, I don't feel all that impoverished, but I try not to buy luxurious items and, although I was traveling quite frequently in the past, I don't do so now.... I do worry more about money now, though. I try to be more frugal and I do not go to the hairdresser as often." Although her adjustments appear to be minor—particularly when compared to high school graduates on very tight household budgets—her immediate association of single motherhood with "impoverishment" indicated a stronger awareness that her living standard could not be taken for granted.

Her primary concern in becoming a single mother, moreover, was not the time she could spend with her son but the financing and quality of his education. In addition to swimming lessons and drawing classes, she proudly told me, he soon would also take up piano lessons. In negotiating child support payments during her judicial divorce, she also made sure that her former husband would make payments until their son's graduation from university. Underlining her goal of providing her son with the best possible education, she had already begun to look into the admissions process to exclusive private elementary schools, which would guarantee attainment of a prestigious university degree. "If it is a matter of ¥400,000 to ¥500,000 [US$3,636—$4546] a year," she confidently told me, "[financing a private school education] won't be a big problem."

Although Yamamoto was comparatively well-off in financial terms, combining full-time employment with her son's needs was a major challenge. As she explains, "I usually do not come back [from work] when my child suddenly gets ill. I just can't take off from work. I think that the underlying assumption [in getting this job] was that I was not going to take off from work because of the child. I think I have to respond to this to a certain degree." She answered to these expectations by paying for expensive babysitting services during emergencies, unable to rely on family or friends. Whenever her son had a fever in the morning, she called the babysitting service, waited for the babysitter to arrive and went to work late, saying "Sorry I am late. I fainted." Moreover, she felt pressured not to publicize her divorce at work. As she confided in me, "Actually, I have only told some people at work. It will eventually spread over time, but as far as possible, I would like to keep a lid on it." To minimize negative effects, she changed her name back to her maiden name only two years after her divorce.

Tanaka and Yamamoto experienced similar pressures in balancing their careers and their children's needs. Yet their priorities in managing this balance differed. Whereas Tanaka paid relatively little attention to her finances, Yamamoto was conscious of the importance of income for maintaining her and her son's class status. Having worked hard to attain her own education and middle-class lifestyle, she was well aware of the fragility of her status and the potential risk of downward mobility as a single mother. Less bound to the ideal of a full-time housewife, Yamamoto invested herself fully in work as a means to ensure a good education for her son. Contrary to the emphasis on maternal care for young children among the middle classes, Yamamoto thus expressed her dedication to her son through her commitment to work—leaving her with little control over her role as a mother.

In contrast to Tanaka and Yamamoto, Kimura Eiko was among the few mothers who emphasized spending most of her time with her children when becoming a single mother. Kimura grew up in an industrial district with two working parents in blue-collar jobs and attended a day care center from a young age. As a child, she felt lonely and deprived of the attention of her mother. As she recounts, "When I was little, I always came back [from school] to an empty home. I really hated that. And if I went to a friend's house, if the mother stayed home, ... you would sometimes get homemade chou-crème or waffles. I always aspired to that."

These childhood experiences left a mark on how she thought about family and motherhood as an adult. In speaking about her relationship with her children, she emphasized the importance of a mother's presence and of her emotional support. Yet, she was also aware of the economic realities she and her parents had faced. She adds: "Although I hated [being alone at home] as a child, I now understand that they worked because they had no money.... So, now I feel grateful."

As a teenager, she quit senior high school and worked part-time for a while, but later returned to finish her high school degree by attending an evening high school. A few months before graduation, she became pregnant and, barely out of school, she married and moved out of her parents' home. Kimura hoped for a happy marriage and family life, envisioning them happily passing their days together. She and her spouse thought she should be a full-time housewife, taking care of her two small children. But soon, here too, economic realities set in. Her husband was in his early twenties and earned barely enough for them to make ends meet. As she says, "We always had debts. But if there is no money, that's alright.... I am used to not having money, since I have always lived without it. I can have soy bean sprouts [*moyashi*, the cheapest source of protein] for breakfast, lunch, and dinner, if necessary. I really have no problem with that." Eventually, they were able to move into a subsidized public housing unit for low-income families, an apartment with two large rooms and a dining kitchen, which significantly improved the family finances.

When her children were in elementary school, her marital relationship deteriorated and she filed for divorce. As a single mother, she was able to keep the public housing unit, which, as a single mother with low or no income, she could rent for as little as ¥2,000 (US$18) a month. Initially, she had felt uncertain about her future after divorce and thus decided to take up work. She recounts: "I wasn't sure whether I could make ends meet. In any case, 'I have to earn money!' I thought." But her friends also explained to her that to get the full amount of the dependent children's allowance, she should try not to have too much income. "If you work too much you get less. It's a delicate balance," she notes. "It's best if you live in a public housing unit, work part-time, and you will be better off than working full-time. I love to go to the ward office and ask [about policies and programs]. I always go and ask a lot of questions." She made ends meet with the dependent children's allowance for single mothers, child support payments, and occasional part-time work.

Her choice to work part-time at first, and to stop working altogether later, she explains, was also guided by her concerns for her children. In particular, she recalled her own loneliness as the child of working parents when considering whether to continue working part-time. Working part-time, she explained, enabled her to participate more easily in the PTA (Parent Teacher Association) of her children's school. PTA meetings are often scheduled on weekdays and in the mornings, making it very difficult for working mothers to participate. Working at night, she pointed out, enabled her to make time for these duties. Quitting her job as a hostess in a bar altogether, moreover, allowed her to dedicate herself to her children more fully. She explains:

> That I stopped working in *mizu shôbai* (nighttime entertainment) was in my view good for the children. Maybe it's just me thinking this way. They come home and say "*tadaima*" (I'm home), and they probably walked home thinking [about their day and such things as] "that teacher really sucks" or that she

argued with another girl. If you can talk to someone [about your day] you can feel relieved.... Once they have told me, they relax and say—"let's have a snack (*oyatsu*)!" .... In this sense, it is great that I can now be there for them.

Although she had much less money to work with than Tanaka or Yamamoto, Kimura was confident in her lifestyle since she had, in her words, always lived without money. She was also familiar with the welfare system and had few qualms about making use of public services. In other words, her disposition toward income and public assistance differed markedly from that of mothers with university degrees. Ironically, it was this more laid-back attitude toward income and living standards, as well as her feelings of deprivation as a child, that allowed her to stress the importance of staying at home, evoking the stereotypical image of a middle-class mother.

Similarly, she dealt with her divorce with much greater ease. She initially felt ashamed and her mother worried about what relatives would think. "The relatives all insisted that I should bear with it a little more. Or they said I should let the children go and remarry. But I convinced them." Among her friends and neighbors, she confidently spoke about her divorce. As she relates, "I told my friends that I divorced and also the other mothers at my children's school. People here are really easygoing and say 'Oh, really?' They do not say, 'Oh, it must be hard.' Instead they say [something unrelated such as], 'It's nice weather today.'" Where Tanaka and Yamamoto felt the pressures of social norms in their social environment and at work, Kimura confidently spread the news of her divorce and changed her name (but not her children's) back to her maiden name, making her divorce noticeable in public and in her immediate environment. Rather than feeling threatened by downward mobility, she was happy to learn that as a single mother she was entitled to receive the dependent children's allowance and could get reduced rates for her water bills. Instead of a source of instability, she saw single motherhood as coming with a number of benefits and greater economic stability.

Single mothers' reproductive practices, in the context of these three narratives stand in a complex relationship to their class origins, resources, and aspirations. They shed light not only on differences in resources and in ideals of motherhood, but also on mothers' active engagement with the maintenance and reproduction of their class status. The family backgrounds of the three women illustrate important class differences in family life and in upbringing as well as in resources upon becoming a single mother. Whereas Tanaka's story reflects the life course of an upper middle-class woman raised by a part-time working mother and professional father and attending an exclusive private school, Kimura's experience of growing up with full-time working parents may be considered as characteristic of the working class. Tanaka not only held a degree from a prestigious private high school, but also received significant support from her parents in finding and financing housing and in coping with emergency childcare when becoming a single mother. As a recent study has found, her experience was not unique: single mothers with a university education receive substantially more support from their parents—in obtaining housing, in providing childcare, and in offering financial help—than do single mothers from less affluent households (Iwata 2001).

Kimura's parents, by contrast, both worked full-time out of economic necessity and had precious little time to devote to their children. Kimura herself completed no more than a high school education and experienced significant financial difficulties during marriage. Here, too, the pattern is typical: according to Iwata's study, single mothers with junior or senior high school degrees are likely to have experienced financial instabilities before and during marriage, an experience that is not present in the life trajectories of university graduates (Iwata 2001). Although her parents lived nearby, Kimura received no significant financial support from them upon becoming a single mother. Her only asset was a subsidized public housing unit for low-income families, which significantly reduced her housing costs.

Yamamoto's story, in turn, reflects the possibilities of social mobility, as she achieved an affluent urban lifestyle despite her petit bourgeois origins. Yet, unlike Tanaka, she had no assets or family support to rely on and was aware of the possibility of downward mobility and of her dependence on her performance at work and the stability of her income. Different class backgrounds provided each of these women with different educational opportunities and very different resources from which to draw as single mothers—parental support and assets, public support, and wage or salaried labor.

The family background and experience of the three mothers did not only provide them with different levels of education and financial resources but also shaped their ideals of motherhood. Tanaka had attended a prestigious high school and university, but also aspired to and was expected to become a full-time housewife. When she later became a teacher and single mother, she could not quite detach herself from the idea that it is best for small children to be taken care of by their mother. Kimura, who understood the hardships of working-class motherhood, dreamed of a carefree family life void of the hardships of her childhood, and wished to devote herself more fully to her children, more than her own mother could. Yamamoto found little appeal in housework or the role of a stay-at-home mother. Instead, having been unable to take family support for higher education for granted, she emphasized the importance of work and income as a key to a middle-class living standard and her role in ensuring the necessary financial resources to afford an appropriate education for her son.

Their approaches to motherhood, while not entirely consistent with the class-specific models of motherhood, reflect important differences in their interpretations of middle-class motherhood. Whereas Tanaka defined ideal motherhood in terms of a mother's presence at home as well as in terms of a suitable education and proper upbringing, without much consideration of finances, Yamamoto emphasized her role in facilitating her son's education primarily in financial terms. Kimura, meanwhile, seemed to take the professional housewife ideal at face value—emphasizing her ability to stay at home but neglecting the financial requirements of a middle-class living standard and children's educational attainment. An expert might easily be able to pick out the "correct" understanding of middle-class motherhood along with the "best" approach and pathway to that end. Here, we can see not simply how there are different types of "middle-class" and "working-class" motherhood, but also how women of different class backgrounds interpret and engage with the dominant ideal of middle-class motherhood in different ways, as a means to assert their social status and their identity as mothers in symbolic and substantial terms.

Indeed, differences in disposition also had an effect on how the mothers in this study approached the balance between, on the one hand, work and income and, on the other, children's education and socialization. In becoming a single parent, they faced similar problems: how to balance work with children's needs and how to ensure a certain level of income as well as support for their children. Resources, of course, played an important role in this setting. Had it not been for the ample financial support from her parents, Tanaka would have had difficulties in managing everyday life with two part-time teaching jobs and a small child. Yamamoto could only invest herself in her job because she could afford expensive babysitting services. And Kimura, in turn, unlike other mothers from low-income families, could make ends meet with a part-time job and government allowances because she had access to subsidized public housing.

But differences in resources cannot fully explain their strategic choices between staying home and earning an income. If maternal care is prized among the middle class, and a sign of affluence, why would Kimura, who had very little income, and not Tanaka, be the one to stay at home? And if dedication to work and the welfare of children is a central aspect of working-class motherhood, why would Yamamoto, who had the highest income, and not Kimura, be the one to invest herself most in her job and career?

Upon closer examination of mothers' reproductive practices, we can identify important differences in their disposition toward motherhood, which shaped their actions. Although neither Tanaka nor Yamamoto pursued the role of a stay-at-home mother, their strategies revealed shared concerns over their children's upbringing and education, which they seemed to see as central to their understanding of the role of the middle-class housewife and full-time or education mother. Tanaka, while not as worried about how to finance her daughter's education, was well aware of prejudices against children attending day care centers and the potential barriers children of single mothers might face in obtaining an exclusive private school education. Tanaka and her friends saw constraints on children's education and on the quality of their upbringing as one of the major concerns associated with single motherhood. Consequently, it was important for her to at least grant a little more time to being with her daughter while the latter was below school age, working part-time rather than full-time. Besides her disposition toward motherhood, her family's financial backing made this an available option. Once her daughter reached school age, then, she shifted into a full-time position so as to be able to earn a better income and pursue a career as a teacher and, similarly to Yamamoto, returned home late every evening.

For Yamamoto, her son's education became a major incentive to prioritize work performance and ensure employment stability, particularly after becoming a single mother. Her concern about financing a middle-class lifestyle and education was not unusual. In fact, a higher proportion of single mothers above the age of forty and with a university degree work concurrently in more than one job (such as a daytime and nighttime job) compared to single mothers with a lower educational attainment, even though university graduates tend to earn more than single mothers with high school degrees (JIL 2003). This tendency can be explained by the low wages of working mothers and high tuition fees needed to send children to cram schools, private schools, and universities. While single parents may have similar educational aspirations for their children as do other parents, their children's actual attainment tends to be lower, often ending with junior or senior high school (Kudomi 1993; Okano and Tsuchiya 1999). If higher educational attainment is a central aspiration and a necessary condition for the reproduction of a middle-class status, it also requires mothers with middle-class aspirations to make income from work a high priority unless they have ample family support. Thus, whereas commitment to work has been identified as a way to accommodate motherhood and work among working-class mothers (Kondo 1990; Roberts 1994), in the case of single mothers such a strategy can become an expression of middle-class ambitions. In other words, when push comes to shove, the central element of middle-class motherhood is not mothers' presence in the home, but rather mothers' role in facilitating their children's academic achievement through financial means as well as through socialization practices.

Kimura's story further underlines class differences in resources and dispositions. Where mothers with middle-class ambitions tended be more concerned about work and income, it was a small number of women who, like Kimura, had lived in low-income households as children and as spouses and had very limited resources, that prioritized time with their children upon becoming single mothers and associated "good motherhood" with stay-at-home motherhood. Kimura had grown up with limited means and had experienced financial hardship during her marriage. This experience allowed her to associate single motherhood with stability rather than decline, as not having money was not a new or worrisome condition. Rather than investing herself in work, she stopped working altogether as a single mother, in order to be able to provide better emotional care and support for her daughters. While cheap housing was a precondition for her to be able to stay at home, a different disposition toward motherhood, children's education, and living standards also made this an available option. Her experience adds an interesting irony to our understanding of motherhood and class. Having grown up with limited means and a laid-back attitude toward public assistance, she was able to enjoy single motherhood as a position of stability and to assert herself as a stay-at-home mother despite her limited means. Yet, although she may have achieved an ideal living standard for herself in fulfilling the housewife ideal, she did not, from the perspective of other mothers, actually achieve this status. Middle-class motherhood, they might argue, is not about waffles and chou-crème, but about children's attainment of degrees from first-rate universities.

Single mothers' approaches to work or motherhood thus reveal important differences in dispositions toward and understandings of motherhood and the professional housewife ideal. And their strategies and actions do not only reflect differences in disposition, but also provide insight into the mechanisms of the reproduction of class. Tanaka and Yamamoto, fearing loss of social status and downward mobility, were not only oriented to a specific ideal of motherhood but were also cognizant of the potential impact of single motherhood on their children's future. Tanaka clearly felt the social repercussions of deviating from the nuclear family norm both for herself and her daughter. To protect her social and cultural capital, she hid her identity as a single mother and attempted to uphold the stay-at-home mother ideal as much as possible. Middle-class mothers like Yamamoto, who were concerned about downward mobility, worried most about their children's educational attainment and often sacrificed their own presence at home for this long-term goal. Kimura also negotiated her identity by investing in stay-at-home motherhood, but cared little about income and education, thus inadvertently contributing to the reproduction of her class status among her children. While she was able to manipulate representations of middle-class motherhood, she lacked the economic and cultural capital—in the form of knowledge and aspirations of social mobility—to actually foster a change in her or her children's class position. A university-educated mother, by contrast, may have seen a cheap public housing unit as an opportunity to make the most out of her salary. Mothers' class-specific dispositions not only informed how they negotiated their identities as single mothers, but also potentially contributed to the reproduction of class differences among their children. Motherhood, in this context, is not merely a lifestyle or gender aspect of class but, in forging children's economic, social, and cultural capital, is also a central element of the dynamics of social class in contemporary Japan.

Conclusion

My goal in this book has been to take a closer look at single mothers' lives during the Heisei recession, and based on their experiences, to contribute to a better understanding of the class dynamics of family life and of the gender dimensions of social class in contemporary Japan. While there are a number of studies that have examined women's attitudes toward marriage, childbirth, and employment during this period, there has been a tendency to focus on highly educated women (Bumpass and Choe 2004; Nagase 2006; Nakano 2011; Nemoto 2008), leaving class differences in women's approaches to marriage, motherhood, and employment largely unexplored. As research elsewhere has shown, however, social class is manifested not only in income and occupational differences, but also in differences in the family and in childhood experiences (Rubin 1976; Stacey 1990) as well as in family lifestyles and parenting practices (Lareau 2003). Research on unmarried single mothers in the United States has also shown how marriage and motherhood take on different meanings in different social and economic circumstances (Edin and Kefalas 2005; Luker 1996; Stack 1974; Steedman 1986). Single mothers, viewed from this perspective, offer a unique window on the class aspects of women's lives, and the gender dimensions of social class. Their life stories offer insight into differences in the conditions of their upbringing, while their struggles to manage life as single mothers highlight the meaning and significance of social class and social achievement from a gender perspective.

FAMILY LIFE, CLASS, AND GENERATION

The stories of the single mothers in this book describe the changing character of Japanese family life from the early postwar period to the Heisei recession, offering insight into the diverse and evolving character of family lifestyles. As we have seen in the stories of the single mothers from the pre-Bubble generation, many university-educated mothers grew up in small towns outside of Tokyo within petit bourgeois families with a family business, affording them the necessary economic resources to enroll at a university. Fathers who successfully engaged in business in a period that brought many new freedoms and opportunities emphasized the importance of embracing change and pursuing innovation rather than pressing their daughters to conform to a specific lifestyle or norm, allowing them to pursue a wide range of new opportunities in education and employment available to their generation. The daughters of men who had lifted themselves up by their own bootstraps in the aftermath of World War II were often driven to engage in new opportunities and to build their own lives, in this case, outside of the confines of the family and community of their upbringing. That they left the country for the city to find employment and establish lives on their own was, in this sense, not necessarily a form of resistance to the lifestyle of their upbringing, but more an extension of their fathers' entrepreneurial spirit. Having grown up in a family where women were not only taking charge of the household but also playing a role in the family business, daughters who studied and gained experience in the modern employment sector may have been very much in line with the pioneering spirit of their fathers. Distinctive about university graduates from the pre-Bubble generation, therefore, is their pursuit of new opportunities and their effort to support themselves and become economically independent by embracing the opportunities generated by a rapidly expanding economy.

This openness toward change and eagerness to pursue employment opportunities in the newly emerging employment sectors was, of course, not limited to the middle class. As agriculture was rapidly declining and being replaced by industrial and service sector jobs, women from less affluent rural and agricultural backgrounds also often left the countryside to pursue factory or office work in the city. While they equally embraced the new employment opportunities provided by the modern sector, their motivations differed. Unlike university graduates, who arrived in the city with stipends from their parents to pay for their studies, high school graduates sought employment to support themselves without the assistance of their parents. In other words, although both university graduates and high school graduates were eager to pursue opportunities in the expanding labor market and to become independent from their parents, high school graduates had more pronounced economic prerogatives for trying to make a living on their own.

Education, employment, and marriage, in this context, also took on new meanings. Raised by a generation that had endured many losses and the unpredictable time of the war and immediate postwar period, many of the pre-Bubble generation saw education as a vehicle for social mobility and economic self-reliance. Moreover, growing up at a time when the postwar Japanese family ideal was yet to take on its hegemonic dimensions, this generation associated "family" with the patriarchal structures of the prewar period and the often unhappy and difficult lives of their mothers. Unlike the Bubble generation, these women appeared considerably more critical of their parents' lifestyles, as they represented past structures that postwar reforms aimed to overcome. Their pursuit of a new type of family lifestyle was not so much driven by a resistance to a gender division of labor as it was informed by an urge to live the equal rights promised to women by the postwar constitution. Discursively speaking, therefore, the pre-Bubble generation forged its life course in a very different kind of setting compared to the Bubble generation, with personal self-reliance and economic independence as the main keys to a bright future.

The Bubble generation's narratives of childhood and youth, by contrast, highlight the centrality of the postwar Japanese family ideal, consisting of a breadwinning salaryman and a professional housewife and mother, as a main point of reference for women's life courses. While its main premises, including a university education, a timely marriage to a salaryman in a lifetime position, and the lifestyle of a housewife and mother, are well documented, the stories of women from the Bubble generation also allow insight into the lived experiences linked to this ideal. In contrast with the previous generation's embrace of social change and social mobility, the Bubble generation's experience of childhood and adolescence appeared dominated by a sense of stability and predictability (Kelly 1993). If women felt pressured to conform to the norm of the married housewife and mother, this may however not simply have been a matter of conforming to "social pressure" and gender norms. Considering women's own agency and independence in pursuing their own goals, it is also important to recognize the social and symbolic meanings associated with the ideal. Even if women's own perspectives on motherhood have changed (Ehara 2000; Ohinata 1988), the status of a married wife and mother constitutes more than a domesticated gender role; it additionally allows women, as mothers and housewives, to gain a certain social recognition for these roles (Hendry 1993; Leblanc 1999). The role of housewife and mother, in this context, is appealing not only because it provides women with the opportunity to dedicate themselves to household and children but, more importantly, because it allows women to claim the status of a married middle-class mother.

The stories of women from the Bubble generation, however, also highlight their struggles to realize the expected life course and idealized family lifestyle. Distinctive about the stories of university graduates from this generation was the boredom associated with the educational and employment opportunities with which they grew up. That is, where their predecessors eagerly embraced the opportunities a higher education would provide, the women university graduates of the Bubble generation expressed a certain lack of orientation, despite the fact that they could take a university education for granted and the EEOL had, at least in theory, greatly improved their employment prospects. Precisely because their lifestyles were dominated by a sense of predictability and taken-for-granted opportunities in education and employment, ensured by a thriving Bubble economy, marriage and motherhood also appeared as a mere milestone on the way to achieving the idealized lifestyle of the married middle-class mother. That is, where the previous generation had to forge new pathways in women's employment and marital relations, the challenge for the Bubble generation was to realize the normative prescriptions of the postwar Japanese family ideal. At a time and in a place where getting married to a salaryman in a timely fashion and leading the predictable lifestyle of the professional housewife separated "winners" from "losers" (Sakai 2003; Yamada 2004), adhering to normative expectations, rather than, for instance, living an independent life as a working single woman, appears as a primary means for status attainment.

The stories of the childhood and youth of high school graduates differed significantly not only in terms of the conditions they described of their upbringing, but also in terms of their relationship to the postwar Japanese family ideal. Unlike university graduates, high school graduates appeared quite aware of differences in their lifestyles compared to the normative middle class and the stratified nature of lifestyles in Japanese society. Where university graduates seemed to feel assured of their family's economic standing and of their own opportunities, high school graduates more often recognized the hardships endured by their parents and of the difficulty of affording a more comfortable life despite their best efforts.

Their stories also show that employment opportunities for high school graduates were becoming increasingly constrained with the bursting of the economic Bubble. In contrast to the previous generation, senior high school graduates from the Bubble generation faced a context not only in which having a high school degree was the very minimum needed to land a job, but also in which finding stable employment was considerably more difficult. High school graduates searching for employment after the collapse of the economic Bubble, as a consequence, predominantly worked in freeter-style part-time jobs with few prospects for promotion or permanent employment. In such a context, the idea of being able to stay at home, supported by a breadwinning husband, was appealing not only because it promised a lifestyle that could be likened to that of the postwar middle-class family, but also because it offered greater comfort and status than the lifestyles of their working mothers. Achieving the male-breadwinner ideal of family, even if one were not married to a highly paid salaryman, would at least allow women to escape the daily grind of dead-end part-time jobs and afford them the possibility of avoiding the hardships of working motherhood. Hence, while some emulated the ideal of the full-time housewife in staying at home, they did so not so much as a means to conform to a middle-class ideal, but more so as an escape from the difficult life of the families in which they were raised.

While exact borderlines of class and class culture may be difficult to delineate at a time when family lifestyles were in flux, the specific living conditions, social and economic opportunities, and family lifestyles of women's upbringing clearly generated different outlooks on marriage, motherhood, education, and employment. Of course, family resources and, in particular, the father's occupation and income played a role in facilitating women's educational attainment. When looking at women's actual employment trajectories, the presence or absence of a college or university education also translated into clear differences in the ability to attain not only a certain level of income, but also a permanent position. However, it was not just their education or financial resources that determined their future pathway. The generational and historical contexts of their upbringing also generated specific discursive fields that contributed to different understandings of education, employment, and marriage. Where the stories of women of the pre-Bubble generation were often framed by the spirit of opportunity and social mobility of those times and by the urge to move beyond the devalued status of the women of their family of origin, the Bubble generation's stories emphasize the role of the married wife and mother as constituting an important yardstick that could confer legitimacy and a considerable sense of social status and achievement. Social mobility, in the case of the latter women's life trajectories, therefore, was not purely a matter of acquiring specific qualifications and resources, but was rather also guided by a specific gendered understanding of social achievement within their particular historical and generational context.

SINGLE MOTHERS, EMPLOYMENT, AND "INDEPENDENCE"

If a woman's social status is closely tied not only to her household income and living standard but also to her lifestyle as a mother, becoming a single mother has, needless to say, no small impact on her social status. Significant about single motherhood in Japan is that it remains closely associated with the hardships and poverty facing many working single mothers and the living conditions they confront in raising children without the presence and support of a husband. Single mothers, in this respect, highlight the consequences of a policy regime that has privileged the male-breadwinner family and encouraged middle-class mothers in particular to become stay-at-home mothers. The wide disparity between the family incomes of households led by single mothers and those with two parents not only indicates a persistent gender gap in earnings but also underscores the barriers women face in forming an autonomous household, independent from marriage and family assistance (Orloff 1993). While the Japanese welfare system has received considerable criticism from a gender perspective, the case of single mothers also highlights the privileges given to married mothers in contrast to divorced and unmarried single mothers (Fujiwara 2005a).

But while there is no doubt about the socioeconomic disadvantages facing single mothers in Japanese society, their life trajectories also pose the question of the key factors that enable some to manage life as a single mother more easily than others. Qualifications and resources, of course, play a role. As we have seen, and as has been shown by statistical trends (JIL 2003), a university degree not only facilitates better and often more stable job opportunities, but also results on average in substantially higher incomes. But educational credentials and income are not a panacea when it comes to earning a family wage and achieving work-life balance as a single mother. As research on women's careers in Japan has shown, permanent jobs in the public sector and family assistance with childcare are more crucial for women's ability to pursue a career-track job than the ability to rely on day care services or credentials alone (Hirao 1999). Also among the single mothers described in the preceding chapters, those able to rely on family support for childcare needs managed considerably better than those who could not rely on family (see also Raymo and Zhou 2012). Achieving a stable job and a high income, therefore, is not just a matter of qualifications and effort, but also a matter of informal resources, which have been shown elsewhere (Edin and Lein 1997) to play a crucial role in supporting low-income single mothers' ability to work. Single mothers from low-income families are, however, less likely to rely on family support (Iwata 2004), meaning that there is not only stratification in women's access to qualifications and financial resources but also in the informal resources that can help manage the work-family balance. The families of high school graduates in this book were often unable to offer support because they themselves were still in the workforce and had few extra resources to share; they also often lacked the space and time to house a daughter and support a grandchild. Instead, high school graduates more often relied on government support, for which university graduates were less likely to be eligible. The majority of high school graduates resided in public housing apartments, which considerably reduced their housing expenses, but did not substantially support their ability to manage the work-family balance or to access better jobs.

Even with these resources, however, balancing work and family and earning a stable income remained a precarious matter. While resources mattered, what appeared to have the most significant impact was not only resources and qualifications, but also women's long-term life and employment trajectories. As we saw in Obuchi Miho's story, the fact that she invested in a qualification as a clerical accountant and settled for a career in a job that was neither personally appealing nor fulfilling but that promised a long-term future allowed her, despite having earned a junior college rather than university degree and having no particular career ambitions, to find employment and earn a good income even above the age of forty. Nakada Ikuko, a high school graduate who gradually worked herself into a similar position in accounting, was also among the few high school graduates to earn a stable and comparably high income even at an older age, despite the fact that she did not receive family assistance and had few resources and credentials. Rather than formal credentials alone, the stories described in this book highlight the relevance and importance of women's employment trajectories in defining their circumstances as single mothers. Those who kept their jobs throughout, or at least invested in a specific qualification and expertise at an early stage, fared considerably better than high school or university graduates who interrupted their employment or who changed occupations upon marriage and childbirth in line with the expected life course of a woman of their generation. Such interruption of employment is however not just a matter of women's own dispositions toward employment. As we have seen in Kato Minako's case a woman's employment trajectory is not something she can always determine entirely on her own; it can also be affected by marriage and family demands. While Kato had received career advice from her parents and had acquired qualifications early on, her marriage disrupted her plans, leading her to abandon her profession and work for her husband's business, which derailed her potential to make the most of the qualifications and skills she had gained over the course of ten years.

An understanding of the income and employment trajectories of single mothers, therefore, requires us to pay closer attention not only to their formal qualifications and income levels as a key to single mothers' financial autonomy and independence, but also to the gendered character of women's employment trajectories, that which makes a linear career much less likely for married women and mothers. Single mothers' difficulties in finding stable employment and earning a family wage is not simply a matter of expending just a little more effort, but also needs to be placed in the context of a social policy regime and employment system that has promoted stay-at-home motherhood as the dominant ideal for women when children are young and yet has also made continued and linear employment the main precondition for earning a family wage.

GENDER, CLASS, AND SOCIAL ACHIEVEMENT

The most significant challenge single mothers face is however not just the economic repercussions of raising children on their own and the trials of working motherhood, but also the implications of their living conditions as single mothers for their role and identity as a mother. Policy and media discourses on single mothers often assume that divorcees and unmarried mothers are abandoning "traditional" norms of marriage and family, yet many of the stories of the single mothers in this book convey rather conventional views of marriage and, if anything, a strong aspiration to the role and identity of a mother, a point that has also been underlined in other research on single mothers (Hertog 2009). Were it not for their commitment to becoming mothers, they would have been unlikely to get married (and divorced) or give birth, becoming as a result divorced or unmarried single mothers. While their marriages may not have worked out, single mothers, if anything, constitute a group of women who, at the very least, have given marriage and motherhood the benefit of the doubt. Their stories of marriage, separation, and single motherhood, therefore, highlight their struggles in pursuing an ideal of marriage and motherhood that is increasingly difficult to realize in a changing economy and society.

While much has been made of women's economic independence as a catalyst of divorce, the stories of single mothers themselves underscore rather the social and structural conditions that are weakening the foundations of marriage. As surveys (IPSS 2010) and women's own narratives both show, marriage is widely conflated by women with the idea of having a family and becoming a mother. As a consequence, the conjugal relationship between spouses has become rather marginal to aspirations of marriage, particularly when marriage takes shape as a consequence of an urge to make the "deadline" of getting married by the age of thirty. In addition, as the idea that men are the main, even if not sole, breadwinners of the family remains a central element of a husband's and father's identity (Tanaka 2009) as well as of women's expectations of marriage, the onset of the recession and the spread of unemployment dealt a further blow to already fragile marriages. That is, if the meaning of having a family is primarily, even if not exclusively, constituted by a woman's ability to become a mother and a man's ability to support the family as its main "pillar" (*daikoku bashira*, see, e.g., Gill 2003), this can lead mothers who are faced with unemployment, debt, gambling, violence, or affairs of their husbands to consider life outside of marriage as a more suitable environment for child-rearing. Discussions of marriage and divorce trends that focus their attention primarily on women's attitudes, choices, and independence not only neglect to consider the other half of the equation—men—but also appear to search for answers to the problems facing women in marriage in women's attitudes, rather than in the structural contradictions that have made it increasingly difficult to realize the marriage ideal of male breadwinner and full-time housewife.

As working mothers with often very low incomes, single mothers face yet another set of challenges to their roles as mothers. Becoming a single mother not only often meant having to manage with limited household finances; the need to support the household and children with their own income from work also had an impact on their roles as mothers. It is here that we can see women's class and gender identities intersect. Single mothers' attempts to find the "best" solution to a situation where both family and work are of high priority but at best very difficult to combine allow us to identify important variations in the meanings, priorities, and practices surrounding motherhood. While some high school graduates saw the personal bond and attention between mother and child of which they felt deprived as children as a key element of "good mothering," university graduates more often underlined their concerns about their children's educational and cultural capital by investing in their early childhood socialization and their education through cram school and extracurricular classes, even if this would mean sacrificing their own presence at home. In so doing, they did not simply reflect class-specific practices but also the specific dispositions behind their ambitions for their children's future. An emphasis on maternal care, as we saw in Kimura's case, was not an ideal with which she was brought up but something she embraced as an ambition and a goal in light of the deprivation she felt as the child of working parents. A strong emphasis on education, in turn, could also be, as we saw in Yamamoto's case, an indication of a mother's own experience of not being able to take a tertiary education for granted and might arise out of a legitimate fear of downward mobility. Maternal practices, in both cases, are not just a matter of personal lifestyles and values; they also express mothers' understandings of the key ingredients necessary to realize their ambitions for their children's future.

Mothers who did not send their children to cram school or university were, however, not necessarily oblivious of the importance of education; they may simply have lacked the financial and cultural capital to do so. Single mothers' ambitions for their children to attend university (38.5%) by far exceeds their own educational attainment (12.1% junior college, 6.9% university; MHLW 2011). Yet, as a recent study by the non-profit organization Single Mother's Forum has shown, even within a sample where university graduates are overrepresented, affording a university education for most of those surveyed seemed hardly feasible and was expected to require reliance on loans, support from grandparents, and a child's own earnings (Single Mothers' Forum 2010). To actually facilitate a higher educational attainment for the child of a single mother, therefore, requires not only the necessary funds, but also a strategic recruitment of formal and informal resources and the necessary cultural capital to invest these limited resources effectively and thereby facilitate children's educational success.

Social class and social achievement, viewed from this perspective, is not only a matter of financial resources, educational credentials, and employment trajectories. Viewed from the perspective of single mothers' experiences, a sense of social achievement is also closely intertwined with the class aspects of the postwar Japanese family ideal. If lifetime employment in a large corporation, home ownership, and the ability to take care of children and a stay-at-home wife symbolizes a man's achievement of a middle-class life, for women the prestige associated with the professional housewife, marriage, and motherhood can also constitute a source of social status and recognition. Motherhood, in this case, is not just a gender role, but also plays a key role in children's upbringing as well as in their success in education and employment and their achievement of a middle-class lifestyle. While single mothers may have diverged from the idealized life course of a married mother and housewife, their stories underscore the centrality of motherhood to their sense of social achievement and their role in the shaping of their children's future.

References

Abe, Aya. 2005. "Kodomo no hinkon" [Children and poverty]. In *Kosodate setai no shakai hoshô*, edited by Kokuritsu shakai hoshô jinkô mondai kenkyujo, 119–42. Tokyo: University of Tokyo Press.
———. 2008. *Kodomo no hinkon* [Children and poverty]. Tokyo: Iwanami Shinsho.
———. 2014. *Kodomo no hinkon II* [Children and poverty II]. Tokyo: Iwanami Shinsho.
Abe, Aya, and Akiko Oishi. 2005. "Boshisetai no keizai jôkyô to shakai hoshô" [The financial situation of single mothers and social security policies]. In *Kosodate setai no shakai hoshô*, edited by Kokuritsu shakai hoshô jinkô mondai kenkyûjo, 143–61. Tokyo: University of Tokyo Press.
Akaishi, Chieko. 2014. *Hitorioya katei* [Single parent households]. Tokyo: Iwanami Shinsho.
Allison, Anne. 1994. *Nightwork: Sexuality, Pleasure, and Corporate Masculinity in a Tokyo Hostess Club*. Chicago: University of Chicago Press.
Aoki, Deborah. 2010. *Widows of Japan*. Melbourne: Transpacific Press.
Aoki, Hideo. 2003. *Gendai nihon no "mienai" hinkon* ["Invisible" poverty in contemporary Japan]. Tokyo: Akashi Shoten.
Bertaux, Daniel, and Isabelle Bertaux-Wiame. 1981. "Life Stories in the Bakers' Trade." In *Biography and Society. The Life History Approach in the Social Sciences*, edited by Daniel Bertaux, 169–90. Beverly Hills, CA: Sage.
Bertaux, Daniel, and Martin Kohli. 1984. "The Life Story Approach: A Continental View." *Annual Review of Sociology* 10: 215–37.
Bertaux, Daniel, and Paul Thompson. 1997. *Pathways to Social Class*. Oxford: Clarendon Press.
Bourdieu, Pierre. 1984. *Distinction. A Social Critique of the Judgment of Taste*. Cambridge, MA: Harvard University Press.
———. 1987. "What Makes a Social Class? On the Theoretical and Practical Existence of Groups." *Berkeley Journal of Sociology* 32: 1–17.
———. 2001. *Masculine Domination*. Stanford, CA: Stanford University Press.
Brinton, Mary C. 1992. "Christmas Cakes and Wedding Cakes: The Social Organization of Japanese Women's Life Course." In *Japanese Social Organization*, edited by Takie Sugiyama Lebra, 79–109. Honolulu: University of Hawaii Press.
———. 1993. *Women and the Economic Miracle*. Berkeley: University of California Press.
———. 2001. "Married Women's Labor in East Asian Economies." In *Women's Working Lives in East Asia*, edited by Mary C. Brinton, 1–37. Stanford, CA: Stanford University Press.
———. 2011. *Lost in Transition*. Cambridge: Cambridge University Press.

Bumpass, Larry L., and Minja Kim Choe. 2004. "Attitudes Relating to Marriage and Family Life." In *Marriage, Work, and Family Life in Comparative Perspective*, edited by Noriko O. Tsuya and Larry L. Bumpass, 19–38. Honolulu: University of Hawaii Press.

Edin, Kathryn, and Maria Kefalas. 2005. *Promises I Can Keep: Why Poor Women Put Motherhood Before Marriage*. Berkeley: University of California Press.

Edin, Kathryn, and Laura Lein. 1997. *Making Ends Meet: How Single Mothers Survive Welfare and Low-Wage Work*. New York: Russell Sage Foundation.

Ehara, Yumiko. 1994. "Kekkon shinai kamoshirenai shôkôgun" [The phenomenon of "maybe I won't get married"]. *Kazoku shakaigaku kenkyû* 6: 37–44.

———. 2000. "Hahaoyatachi no double bind" [The double bind of mothers]. In *Shoshika jidai no gender to hahaoya ishiki*, edited by Yoriko Meguro and Sumiko Yazawa, 29–46. Tokyo: Shin'yosha.

———. 2004. "Gender ishiki no henyô to kekkon kaihi" [Changes in gender consciousness and marriage avoidance]. In *Shoshika no gender bunseki*, edited by Yoriko Meguro, 27–50. Tokyo: Keisô Shobô.

Esping-Andersen, Gøsta. 1990. *The Three Worlds of Welfare Capitalism*. Princeton, NJ: Princeton University Press.

———. 1999. *Social Foundations of Postindustrial Economies*. Oxford: Oxford University Press.

Ezawa, Aya. 2006. "How Japanese Single Mothers Work." *Japanstudien* 18: 57–82.

Ezawa, Aya, and Chisa Fujiwara. 2005. "Lone Mothers and Welfare-to-Work Policies in Japan and the United States: Toward an Alternative Perspective." *Journal of Sociology and Social Welfare* 32 (4): 41–63.

Field, Norma. 1995. "The Child as Laborer and Consumer: The Disappearance of Childhood in Contemporary Japan." In *Children and the Politics of Culture*, edited by Sharon Stephens, 51–78. Princeton, NJ: Princeton University Press.

Fraser, Nancy, and Linda Gordon. 1994. "A Genealogy of *Dependency*: Tracing a Keyword of the U.S. Welfare State." *Signs* 19 (2): 309–36.

Fujii, Harue. 2002. *Sengyô shufu wa ima* [Professional housewives today]. Kyoto: Minerva Shobô.

Fujimoto, Kayo. 2004. "Feminine Capital: The Forms of Capital in the Female Labor Market in Japan." *Sociological Quarterly* 45 (1): 91–111.

Fujiwara, Chisa. 1997. "Boshisetai no shotokuhoshô to jidô fuyô teate" [Single mothers' income security and the dependent children's allowance]. *Josei to rôdô 21* 6 (23): 6–28.

———. 2005a. "Fukushi to joseirôdô kyôkyû no kankeishi" [The history of the relationship between welfare and women's labor supply]. In *Fukushi shakai no rekishi*, edited by Kazuro Saguchi and Kiyoshi Nakagawa, 109–44. Kyoto: Minerva Shobô.

———. 2005b. "Hitori oya no shûgyô to kaisôsei" [Class aspects of work patterns of single parents]. *Shakai seisaku gakkai zasshi* [Journal of the Society of the Study of Social Policy] 13: 161–75.

Fuse, Akiko. 1984. *Atarashî kazoku no sôzô* [Imagining the new family]. Tokyo: Aoki Shoten.

Fuwa, Makiko. 2013. "Work-Family Conflict and Attitudes Toward Marriage." *Journal of Family Issues* 35: 731–54.

Gelb, Joyce, and Margarita Estevez-Abe. 1998. "Political Women in Japan: A Case Study of the Seikatsusha Network Movement." *Social Science Japan Journal* 1 (2): 263–79.

Genda, Yuji. 2005. *A Nagging Sense of Job Insecurity*. Tokyo: International House of Japan.

Gill, Tom. 2003. "When Pillars Evaporate: Structuring Masculinity on the Japanese Margins." In *Men and Masculinities in Contemporary Japan*, edited by James E. Roberson and Nobue Suzuki, 144–61. London: RoutledgeCurzon.

———. 2011. "Failed Manhood in the Streets of Urban Japan: The Meanings of Self-Reliance for Homeless Men." In *Recreating Japanese Men*, edited by Sabine Frühstück and Anne Walthall, 177–97. Berkeley: University of California Press.

Goldstein-Gideoni, Ofra. 2012. *Housewives of Japan*. New York: Palgrave Macmillan.

Gordon, Andrew. 1997. "Managing the Japanese Household: The New Life Movement in Postwar Japan." *Social Politics* 4 (2): 245–83.

Hara, Junsuke, and Kazuo Seiyama. 2005 [1999]. *Inequality amid Affluence: Social Stratification in Japan*. Melbourne: Transpacific Press.
Harada, Sumitaka. 1988. "'Nihongata fukushi shakai'ron no kazokuzô" [The family ideal in the discourse on the Japanese-style welfare society]. In *Tenkanki no fukushi kokka*, edited by University of Tokyo Institute of Social Science, 303–91. Tokyo: University of Tokyo Press.
Hasegawa, Yutaka. 2014. *Kakusa shakai ni okeru kazoku no seikatsu/kosodate/kyôiku to arata na kon'nan* [Recent issues in family life, child-rearing, and education in an unequal society]. Tokyo: Junposha.
Hayashi, Chiyo. 1992. *Boshiryô no sengoshi* [A postwar history of mother-and-child-dormitories]. Tokyo: Domesu Shuppan.
Hendry, Joy. 1993. "The Role of the Professional Housewife." In *Japanese Women Working*, edited by Janet Hunter, 224–41. London: Routledge.
Hertog, Ekatarina. 2009. *Tough Choices: Bearing an Illegitimate Child in Japan*. Stanford, CA: Stanford University Press.
Hertog, Ekaterina, and Miho Iwasawa. 2011. "Marriage, Abortion, or Unwed Motherhood? How Women Evaluate Alternative Solutions to Premarital Pregnancies in Japan and the United States." *Journal of Family Issues* 32: 1674–99.
Higuchi, Yoshio, and Kiyoshi Ota, eds. 2004. *Joseitachi no heisei fukyo* [Women and the Heisei recession]. Tokyo: Nihon Keizai Shinbunsha.
Hirao, Keiko. 1999. "Josei no shoki career keisei ni okeru rôdôshijô e no teichakusei" [Women's attachment to the labor market at the early stages of their career formation]. *Nihon rôdô kenkyû zasshi* 471: 29–41.
Holloway, Susan D. 2010. *Women and Family in Contemporary Japan*. Cambridge, UK: Cambridge University Press.
Honda, Yuki. 2000. "'Kyôiku mama'no zon'ritsu jijô" [The conditions of existence of "education mothers"]. In *Oya to ko: kôsaku suru life course*, edited by Hiroko Fujisaki, 159–82. Kyoto: Minerva Shobô.
———. 2004. "'Hi-kyôiku mama' tachi no shozai" [The situation of "non-educating" mothers]. In *Josei no shûgyô to oyako kankei*, edited by Yuki Honda, 167–84. Tokyo: Keisô Shobô.
Huppatz, Kate. 2009. "Reworking Bourdieu's 'Capital': Feminine and Female Capitals in the Field of Paid Caring Work." *Sociology* 43 (1): 45–66.
Imamura, Anne. 1987. *Urban Japanese Housewives*. Honolulu: University of Hawaii Press.
Inoue, Tetsuo. 1956. "Sengo jûnen no boshi fukushi" [Ten years of postwar maternal and child welfare]. *Shakai Jigyô* 39 (3): 18–28.
IPSS (National Institute of Population and Social Security Research). 2010. "Dai 14 kai shussei dôkô kihon chôsa: kekkon to shussan ni kan suru zenkoku chôsa: dokushinsha chôsa kekka no gaiyô" [Report on the Fourteenth Japanese National Fertility Survey: Attitudes toward Marriage among Japanese Singles]. Tokyo: National Institute of Population and Social Security Research.
———. 2012. *Jinkô tôkei shiryôshu* [Vital Statistics Data]. Tokyo: National Institute of Population and Social Security Research.
Ishida, Hiroshi. 1993. *Social Mobility in Contemporary Japan*. Stanford, CA: Stanford University Press.
Ishida, Hiroshi, and David Slater. 2010. "Social Class in Japan." In *Social Class in Japan: Structures, Sorting, and Strategies*, edited by Hiroshi Ishida and David Slater, 1–29. London: Routledge.
Iwai, Hachiro, and Rinko Manabe. 2000. "M-jigata shûgyô patân no teichaku to sono imi" [The hardening of the M-shaped work pattern and its meaning]. In *Nihon no kaisô system 4: jendâ/shijô/kazoku*, edited by Kazuo Seiyama, 67–91. Tokyo: University of Tokyo Press.
Iwata, Mika. 2001. "Ribetsu boshikazoku to shinzoku no shien: hahaoya no gakureki kara mita kaisôsei" [Family support for divorced single-mother families: considering social class from the perspective of mothers' educational attainment]. *Kyôiku fukushi kenkyû* 7: 57–72.
———. 2004. "Boshi setai no kaisôsei—shigen to seiyaku to riyô no shiten kara" [Class aspects of single motherhood: viewed from the perspective of the limits and use of resources]. *Kyôiku fukushi kenkyû* 10 (1): 5–22.

Japan High Court. 2012. "The Annual Report of Judicial Statistics." Tokyo: General Secretariate, High Court.
JIL (Japan Institute of Labor). 2003. *Boshisetai no haha e no shûrôshien ni kan suru kenkyû* [Research on work support for mothers in lone-mother households]. Tokyo: Japan Institute of Labor.
———. 2013. "Kosodate to shigoto no hazama ni iru joseitachi" [Women between work and child-rearing]. Tokyo: Japan Institute of Labor.
Jolivet, Muriel. 1997. *Japan: The Childless Society?* New York and London: Routledge.
Kamano, Saori. 2004a. "Dokushin danjô no kaku kekkonzô" [Images of marriage among single men and women]. In *Shoshika no gender bunseki*, edited by Yoriko Meguro and Hachiro Nishoka, 78–106. Tokyo: Keisô Shobô.
———. 2004b. "Dokushin josei no kekkon iyoku to shussan iyoku" [The desire to marry and give birth among single women]. In *Shoshika no gender bunseki*, edited by Yoriko Meguro, 107–23. Tokyo: Keisô Shobô.
Kamata, Toshiko. 1987. *Tenki ni tatsu josei rôdô* [Women's work in times of change]. Tokyo: Gakubunsha.
Kanbara, Fumiko. 1991. *Gendai no kekkon to fûfû kankei* [Marriage and marital relations in contemporary Japan]. Tokyo: Baifûkan.
———. 2000a. "Kazoku kaisô to kosodate" [Family, social class, and child-rearing]. In *Kyôikuki no kosodate to oyakokankei*, edited by Fumiko Kanbara, 146–68. Kyoto: Minerva Shobô.
———. 2000b. *Kyôiku to kazoku no fubyôdô mondai* [The problem of inequality in education between families]. Tokyo: Koseisha Koseikaku.
Kariya, Takehiko. 2001. *Kaisôka nihon to kyôiku kiki* [Education in crisis in stratified Japan]. Tokyo: Yushindô.
———. 2010. "From Credential Society to 'Learning Capital' Society: A Rearticulation of Class Formation in Japanese Education and Society." In *Social Class in Contemporary Japan*, edited by Hiroshi Ishida and David Slater, 87–113. London and New York: Routledge.
Kasuga, Kisuyo. 1989. *Fushikatei o ikiru* [Life as a single father]. Tokyo: Keisô Shobô.
Kawaguchi, Emiko. 2003. *Senso mibôjin: higai to kagai no hazama de* [War widows: between victim and perpetrator]. Tokyo: Domesu Shuppan.
Kelly, William W. 1993. "Finding a Place in Metropolitan Japan." In *Postwar Japan as History*, edited by Andrew Gordon, 189–216. Berkeley: University of California Press.
Kilkey, Majiella, and Jonathan Bradshaw. 1999. "Lone Mothers, Economic Well-Being, and Policies." In *Gender and Welfare State Regimes*, edited by Diane Sainsbury, 147–84. Oxford: Oxford University Press.
Kimoto, Kimiko. 1995. *Kazoku/gender/kigyôshakai* [Family, gender, corporate society]. Kyoto: Minerva Shobô.
———. 2000. "Kigyôshakai no henka to kazoku" [Changes in corporate society and the family]. *Kazoku shakaigaku kenkyû* 12 (1): 27–40.
Kodomo no hinkon hakusho henshû înkai, ed. 2009. *Kodomo no hinkon hakusho* [White paper on child poverty]. Tokyo: Akashi Shoten.
Kondo, Dorinne K. 1990. *Crafting Selves*. Chicago: University of Chicago Press.
Konishi, Yuma. 2003. "Hinkon to kodomo" [Children and poverty]. In *Gendai nihon no "mienai" hinkon*, edited by Hideo Aoki, 85–109. Tokyo: Akashi Shoten.
Kudomi, Yoshiyuki. 1993. *Yutakasa no teihen ni ikiru* [Living on the lower ranges of affluence]. Tokyo: Aoki Shoten.
Kurotani, Sawa. 2014. "Working Women of the Bubble Generation." In *Capturing Contemporary Japan*, edited by Satsuki Kawano, Glenda S. Roberts, and Susan Orpett Long, 83–104. Honolulu: University of Hawaii Press.
Lareau, Annette. 2003. *Unequal Childhoods: Class, Race, and Family Life*. Berkeley: University of California Press.
Lawler, Steph. 1999. "'Getting Out and Getting Away': Women's Narratives of Class Mobility." *Feminist Review* 63: 3–24.

References

Leblanc, Robin M. 1999. *Bicycle Citizens: The Political World of the Japanese Housewife.* Berkeley: University of California Press.
Lovell, Terry. 2000. "Thinking Feminism with and against Bourdieu." *Feminist Theory* 1 (11): 11–32.
Luker, Kristin. 1996. *Dubious Conceptions: The Politics of Teenage Pregnancy.* Cambridge, MA: Harvard University Press.
McCall, Leslie. 1992. "Does Gender Fit? Bourdieu, Feminism, and Conceptions of Social Order." *Theory and Society* 21 (6): 837–67.
McLeod, Julie. 2005. "Feminists Re-Reading Bourdieu: Old Debates and New Questions about Gender Habitus and Gender Change." *Theory and Research in Education* 3 (11): 11–30.
McNay, Lois. 1999. "Gender, Habitus, and the Field: Pierre Bourdieu and the Limits of Reflexivity." *Theory, Culture & Society* 16: 95–116.
Meguro, Yoriko, and Hirotoshi Shibata. 1999. "Kigyôshugi to kazoku" [Corporatism and the family]. In *Kôza Shakaigaku: 2 Kazoku*, edited by Yoriko Meguro and Hideki Watanabe, 59–88. Tokyo: University of Tokyo Press.
MEXT (Ministry of Education, Culture, Sports, Science, and Technology). 2006. "Monbu kagaku tôkei yôran" [Statistical Abstract of Education, Science, and Culture]. Tokyo: Ministry of Education, Culture, Sports, Science, and Technology.
———. 2008. "Kodomo no gakkôgai de no gakushû katsudô ni kan suru jittai chôsa hôkoku." Tokyo: Ministry of Education, Culture, Sports, Science, and Technology.
MHLW (Ministry of Health, Labor, and Welfare). 2004. "Jinkô dôtai tôkei" [Vital Statistics].
———. 2008. "Zenkoku boshi setai tô chôsa kekka hôkoku" [National Survey of Fatherless Families]. Tokyo: Ministry of Health, Labor, and Welfare.
———. 2011. "Zenkoku boshi setai tô chôsa kekka hôkoku" [National Survey of Fatherless Families]. Tokyo: Ministry of Health, Labor, and Welfare.
———. 2012a. "Heisei 24 nen hihogosha chôsa" [National Survey on Public Assistance Recipients 2012]. Tokyo: Ministry of Health, Labor, and Welfare.
———. 2012b. "Heisei 24 nen hihogosha chôsa" [National Survey of Public Assistance Recipients 2012]. Tokyo: Ministry of Health, Labor and Welfare.
———. 2013a. "Heisei 25 nen kokumin seikatsu kiso chôsa" [Comprehensive Survey of Living Conditions 2012]. Tokyo: Ministry of Health, Labor, and Welfare.
———. 2013b. "Jinkô dôtai tôkei" [Vital Statistics]. Tokyo: Ministry of Health, Labor, and Welfare.
MHW (Ministry of Health and Welfare). 1952. "Zenkoku boshi setai chôsa kekka hôkokusho" [National Survey of Fatherless Families]. Tokyo: Ministry of Health and Welfare, Children and Families Bureau
———. 1956. "Zenkoku boshi setai chôsa kekka hôkokusho" [National Survey of Fatherless Families]. Tokyo: Ministry of Health and Welfare, Children and Families Bureau.
———. 1959. *Jidôfukushi 10 nen no ayumi* [Ten years of child welfare]. Tokyo: Ministry of Health and Welfare, Children and Families Bureau.
———. 1987. "Jidô fuyô teatehô tokubetsu fuyô teate nado no shikyû ni kan suru hôritsu no kaishaku to un'yô" [Interpretation and implementation of the law regarding the distribution of the dependent children's allowance and special care allowance]. Tokyo: Ministry of Health and Welfare, Children and Family Bureau.
MIC (Ministry of Internal Affairs and Communications). 2010. *Heisei 22 nen kokusei chôsa hôkoku* [Population Census 2000]. Tokyo: Ministry of Internal Affairs and Communications.
———. 2015. "Nihon no tôkei" [Japan Statistical Yearbook]. Tokyo: Ministry of Internal Affairs and Communications.
Miura, Mari. 2012. *Welfare through Work: Conservative Ideas, Partisan Dynamics, and Social Protection in Japan.* Ithaca: Cornell University Press.
Murakami, Kimiko. 1987. *Senryoki no fukushi seisaku* [Welfare policies during the Occupation]. Tokyo: Keisô Shobô.
Nagase, Nobuko. 2006. "Japanese Youth's Attitudes towards Marriage and Child Rearing." In *The Changing Japanese Family*, edited by Ayumi Takenaka and Marcus Rebick, 39–53. London: Routledge.

Nakada, Teruko, Kiyoe Sugimoto, and Akemi Morita. 2001. *Nichibei no shinguru fazâ tachi* [Single fathers in the United States and Japan]. Kyoto: Minerva Shobô.
Nakano, Lynne. 2011. "Working and Waiting for an 'Appropriate Person.'" In *Home and Family in Japan*, edited by Richard Ronald and Allison Alexy, 131–51. London: Routledge.
"Nakusô! Kodomo no hinkon" zenkoku network, ed. 2012. *Daishinsai to kodomo no hinkon hakushô* [The white paper on child poverty and the Great Northeastern Earthquake]. Tokyo: Kamogawa Shuppan.
Nemoto, Kumiko. 2008. "Postponed Marriage: Exploring Women's Views of Matrimony and Work in Japan." *Gender and Society* 22 (2): 219–37.
Nonaka, Ikuko. 1987. "Rikon, soshite henshin" [My transformation after divorce]. *Boshi fukushi* 37 (345): 4–5.
Ochiai, Emiko. 1994. *21 Seiki no Kazoku e* [The Japanese Family System in Transition]. Tokyo: Yuhikaku Sensho.
OECD (Organisation for Economic Co-operation and Development). 2006. "Economic Survey of Japan 2006: Income Inequality, Poverty, and Social Spending." Paris: OECD.
———. 2011. *Doing Better for Families*. Paris: OECD.
———. 2013. "Economic Survey of Japan 2013." Paris: OECD.
Ogasawara, Yuko. 1998. *Office Ladies and Salaried Men: Power, Gender, and Work in Japanese Companies*. Berkeley: University of California Press.
Ohinata, Masami. 1988. *Bosei no Kenkyû* [Research on motherhood]. Tokyo: Kawashima Shoten.
Okano, Kaori, and Mononori Tsuchiya. 1999. *Education in Contemporary Japan*. Cambridge: Cambridge University Press.
Ono, Hiromi. 2010. "The Socio-Economic Status of Women and Children in Japan: Comparisons with the USA." *International Journal of Law, Policy, and the Family* 24 (2): 171–76.
Orloff, Ann Shola. 1993. "Gender and the Social Rights of Citizenship: The Comparative Analysis of Gender Relations and Welfare States." *American Sociological Review* 58: 303–28.
Osawa, Machiko. 1999. "Shigoto to katei no chôwa no tame no shûgyô shien" [Work support for harmony between work and family]. *Kikan shakai hoshô kenkyû* [The Quarterly of Social Security Research] 34 (4): 385–91.
Osawa, Mari. 1993. *Kigyôchûshinshakai o koete* [Beyond a corporate-centered society]. Tokyo: Jijitsushinsha.
———. 2002. "Twelve Million Full-Time Housewives: The Gender Consequences of Japan's Postwar Social Contract." In *Social Contracts under Stress*, edited by Olivier Zunz, Leonard Schoppa, and Nobuhiro Hiwatari, 255–77. New York: Russell Sage Foundation.
Oshio, Mayumi. 1996. *Kazokuteate no kenkyû* [Research on the family allowance]. Tokyo: Hôritsu Bunkasha.
Partner, Simon. 1999. *Assembled in Japan: Electrical Goods and the Making of the Japanese Consumer*. Berkeley: University of California Press.
Peng, Ito. 1997. "Single Mothers in Japan: Unsupported Mothers Who Work." In *Single Mothers in an International Context: Mothers or Workers?* edited by Simon Duncan and Rosalind Edwards, 115–48. London: UCL Press.
Raymo, James M., and Miho Ishikawa. 2005. "Marriage Market Mismatches in Japan: An Alternative View of the Relationship between Women's Education and Marriage" *American Sociological Review* 70 (5): 801–22.
Raymo, James M., Miho Iwasawa, and Larry L. Bumpass. 2004. "Marital Dissolution in Japan: Recent Trends and Patterns." *Demographic Research* 11 (14): 395–420.
Raymo, James M., and Hiromi Ono. 2007. "Coresidence With Parents, Women's Economic Resources, and the Transition to Marriage in Japan." *Journal of Family Issues* 28 (5): 653–81.
Raymo, James M., Hyunjoon Park, Miho Iwasawa, and Yanfei Zhou. 2014. "Single Motherhood, Living Arrangements, and Time with Children in Japan." *Journal of Marriage and the Family* 76: 843–61.
Raymo, James M., and Yanfei Zhou. 2012. "Living Arrangements and the Well-Being of Single Mothers in Japan." *Population Research and Policy Review* 31: 727–49.

Reay, Diane. 2004. "Gendering Bourdieu's Concept of Capitals? Emotional Capital, Women, and Social Class." In *Feminism after Bourdieu*, edited by Lisa Adkins and Beverly Skeggs, 57–74. Oxford: Blackwell.
Roberson, James E., and Nobue Suzuki. 2003. "Introduction." In *Men and Masculinities in Contemporary Japan*, edited by James E. Roberson and Nobue Suzuki, 1–19. London and New York: RoutledgeCurzon.
Roberts, Glenda S. 1994. *Staying on the Line: Blue Collar Women in Contemporary Japan*. Honolulu: University of Hawaii Press.
Rohlen, Thomas P. 1974. *For Harmony and Strength*. Berkeley: University of California Press.
Rosenbluth, Frances McCall. 2007. *The Political Economy of Japan's Low Fertility*. Stanford, CA: Stanford University Press.
Rubin, Lillian B. 1976. *Worlds of Pain. Life in the Working Class Family*: Basic Books.
Sakai, Junko. 2003. *Makeinu no Toboe* [The howling of the loser dogs]. Tokyo: Kodansha.
Sato, Toshiki. 2000. *Fubyôdô shakai nihon* [Japan as an unequal society]. Tokyo: Chûkô Shinsho.
Shimoebisu, Miyuki. 1994. "Kazoku seisaku no rekishiteki tenkai. Ikuji ni taisuru seisaku taiô no hensen" [The historical development of family policies: changes in childcare policies]. In *Gendai kazoku to shakai hoshô*, edited by Shakai hoshô kenkyûjo, 251–72. Tokyo: University of Tokyo Press.
———. 2008. *Yoiku seisaku ni miru kokka to kazoku: boshisetai no shakaigaku* [Family, State, and Child Support Policy]: Keisô Shobô.
Shirahase, Sawako. 2005. *Shoshi korei shakai no mienai kakusa: gender, sedai, kaisô no yukue* [Unseen gaps in an aging society: Locating gender, generation, and class in Japan]. Tokyo: University of Tokyo Press.
———. 2010. "Marriage as an Association of Social Classes in a Low Fertility Rate Society: Towards a New Theory of Social Stratification." In *Social Class in Contemporary Japan*, edited by Hiroshi Ishida and David Slater, 57–83. London and New York: Routledge.
Silva, Elizabeth B. 2005. "Gender, Home, and Family in Cultural Capital Theory." *British Journal of Sociology* 56 (1):83–103.
Single Mothers' Forum. 2010. "Boshikatei no kodomo to kyôiku: boshi katei no kodomo no kyôiku jittai to intabyû hôkokusho" [The education of single mothers' children: an interview report regarding the educational situation of children of single mothers]. Tokyo: Single Mothers' Forum.
Skeggs, Beverly. 1997. *Formations of Class and Gender: Becoming Respectable*. London: Sage.
Stacey, Judith. 1990. *Brave New Families: Stories of Domestic Upheaval in Late-Twentieth-Century America*. Berkeley: University of California Press.
Stack, Carol. 1974. *All Our Kin*. New York: Harper and Row.
Steedman, Carolyn. 1986. *Landscape for a Good Woman: A Story of Two Lives*. London: Virago.
Tachibanaki, Toshiaki. 2005. *Confronting Income Inequality in Japan*. Cambridge, MA: MIT Press.
———. 2008. *Jojo kakusa* [Inequality among women]. Tokyo: Tôyô Keizai Shinpôsha.
Takahashi, Mutsuko. 1997. *The Emergence of Welfare Society in Japan*. Adershot, UK: Avebury.
Tanaka, Toshiyuki. 2009. *Danseigaku no shintenkai* [New developments in Men's Studies]. Tokyo: Seikyusha.
Tendo, Mutsuko. 2003. "Shoshika to wa donna mondai ka" [What is the problem of the fertility decline?]. In *Toshi kankyô to kosodate*, edited by Sumiko Yazawa, Mutsuko Tendo, and Yoko Kunihiro, 13–38. Tokyo: Keisô Shobô.
Tsuru, Tamiko, ed. 2012. *"Tairyô shitsugyô shakai" no rôdô to kazoku seikatsu* [Labor and family life in a "society with high unemployment"]. Tokyo: Ôtsuki Shoten.
Uzuhashi, Takafumi. 1997a. *Gendai fukushikokka no kokusai hikaku* [An international comparison of contemporary welfare states]. Tokyo: Nihon hyôronsha.

———. 1997b. "One parent family o meguri kokusaiteki dôkô to kôteki seisaku" [International trends regarding one-parent families and public policy]. *Kikan kakei keizai kenkyû* 33 (1): 9–19.

Vogel, Ezra F. 1963. *Japan's New Middle Class*. Berkeley: University of California Press.

Vogel, Suzanne H. 1978. "Professional Housewife: The Career of Urban Middle-Class Japanese Women." *Japan Interpreter* 12 (1):16–43.

White, Gordon, and Roger Goodman. 1998. "Welfare Orientalism and the Search for an East Asian Welfare Model." In *The East Asian Welfare Model*, edited by Roger Goodman, Gordon White, and Huck-ju Kwon, 3–24. London: Routledge.

White, Merry. 1987. "The Virtue of Japanese Mothers: Cultural Definitions of Women's Lives." *Daedalus* 116 (3): 149–63.

———. 2002. *Perfectly Japanese: Making Families in an Era of Upheaval*. Berkeley: University of California Press.

Yamada, Masahiro. 1999. *Parasite single no jidai* [The era of parasite singles]. Tokyo: Chikuma Shinsho.

———. 2000. "Kekkon no genzai teki imi" [The contemporary meaning of marriage]. In *Kekkon to partner kankei*, edited by Kyoko Yoshizumi, 56–80. Kyoto: Minerva Shobô.

———. 2004. *Kibô kakusa shakai* [A society of unequal hope]. Tokyo: Chikuma Shobô.

Yamataka, Shigeri. 1977. *Boshifukushi yonjûnen* [Forty years of mother-and-child welfare]. Tokyo: Shôbunsha.

———. 1982. *Waga shiawase wa waga te de* [Happiness by our own hands]. Tokyo: Domesu Shuppan.

Yazawa, Sumiko, Yoko Kunihiro, and Mutsuko Tendo. 2003. "Wakai hahaoya no 'haha identity'" [Young mothers' identities as mothers]. In *Toshi kankyo to kosodate*, edited by Sumiko Yazawa, Yoko Kunihiro, and Mutsuko Tendo, 97–113. Tokyo: Keisô Shobô.

Yokoyama, Fumino. 2002. *Sengo nihon no josei seisaku* [Postwar Japanese women's policies]. Tokyo: Keisô Shobo.

Yoshizumi, Kyoko. 1997. *"Kindai kazoku"o koeru* [Beyond the "modern family"]. Tokyo: Aoki Shoten.

Index

Bourdieu, Pierre, xvii
Bubble generation, the, 36, 37, 109; attitudes toward marriage among, 36, 46–50, 50, 52–53, 59; conjugal relations among, 46–47, 49, 53, 54–56; educational attainment of, 36, 38, 39–41, 109; employment among, 42–45, 53, 110; family ideal of, 46, 49, 50, 109; high school graduates among, 38–41, 42–43, 47–49, 110; housewife ideal and, 49, 109; marriage timing of, 46–47, 47; motherhood and, 47, 48, 49, 51, 56, 58–59, 109; social status and social achievement among, 46, 47, 49, 50, 109, 110; working motherhood and, 51; university graduates among, 38, 44–45, 46–47, 109; unmarried mothers among, 56–59. *See also* pre-Bubble generation; single mothers

child support payments, 14, 67–68
cultural capital, xvii, xix, 5–6, 80, 102–105; gender and, xviii, 89, 95

Daily Life Security Law, xv, xvi
day care centers, public, 4, 6, 7, 13, 30, 67–68, 69–70, 71, 72, 72–73, 74, 78, 90, 91–92, 96, 99
dependent children's allowance (*jidô fuyô teate*), xvi, 13, 16, 67–68, 69, 70, 71, 75, 76, 77, 100

divorce, xiv, 54–56, 62, 63, 98, 101

economic independence, 11, 29–32, 53, 68–72, 111–113
education mothers (*kyôiku* mama), xxiv, 2, 5, 36, 49, 103
educational attainment, women's, 6, 19, 34, 38. *See also* Bubble generation; pre-Bubble generation; single mothers
employment, gender aspects of, 7, 8, 10, 19, 26, 42, 72–77, 81, 111–113. *See also* Bubble generation; pre-Bubble generation; single mothers
Equal Employment Opportunities Law, 8, 26, 44, 109

family ideal, postwar Japanese, xi, xiii, 1, 2, 36, 37–38, 108–109; class dimensions of, 5–6, 16, 39, 107, 109, 115; contradictory aspects of, 12, 54, 56, 59, 109, 113; policy reinforcement of, 6–8, 111. *See also* Bubble generation; housewife; salaryman
fertility, decline of, xxiii, 7, 9
Fujiwara, Chisa, 94

Hasegawa, Yutaka, 5
Hendry, Joy, 2
Hertog, Ekaterina, 56
Honda, Yuki, 5

housewife, full-time, xii, xiii, xix, 1, 2–4, 10; company practices and, 3, 7–8; role of, 2, 3–4, 4; social policy and, xii, 6; status of, 1, 4, 6, 8, 36, 37, 102, 105. *See also* family ideal; salaryman

Iwata, Mika, 102

Kariya, Takehiko, 5
Kondo, Dorinne, 4
Konishi, Yuma, 5
Kudomi, Yoshiyuki, 5

life history research, social class and, xii, xx–xxi

marriage, attitudes toward, 9–10, 114; class dimensions of, 11; economic benefits of, 11; trends in, 9. *See also* Bubble generation; pre-Bubble generation
mother-and-child homes (*boshiryô*), xvi
motherhood, class aspects of, xviii–xix, 4, 101–105, 114–115; employment and, 10; middle-class, xix, 2–4, 93, 104; working-class, xviii, 4, 93. *See also* Bubble generation; pre-Bubble generation; single mothers
Motherhood Protection Law, xv

National Widow's Group Association, xv
never-married single mothers. *See* unmarried single mothers

Ogasawara, Yuko, 3
Osawa, Mari, 7

parasite singles, 11
poverty, xi; among single mothers, xii, xiv, xvii, 12, 68, 111
Postwar Japanese Family System, 6, 9
pre-Bubble generation, the, 18, 20, 107–108; attitudes toward marriage among, 29–34; educational attainment of, 19–23, 24–25, 107, 108; employment among, 26–29, 30, 107–108; gender relations among, 23–24, 108; high school graduates among, 20–21, 26, 29–31, 108;
motherhood and, 32–34; social mobility and, 20, 25, 34; university graduates among, 21–25, 27–29, 31–34, 107. *See also* Bubble generation
professional housewife. *See* housewife
public assistance, xvi, 12, 40, 64, 67–68, 78–80, 85
public housing, 13, 63, 66, 79

remarriage, xvii
Roberts, Glenda, 4

salaryman, postwar ideal of, xi, 1, 6, 7, 36, 37
separate last names (*fûfû bessei*), 52
shotgun marriages (*dekichatta kekkon*), xxi, 32, 57
single mothers, xiii, xiv, xxi; co-residence with parents among, 15, 62–63, 71–72, 112; downward mobility among,; 5.76educational attainment of xii, xiii, xxiii, 12, 16, 65, 90, 96, 99xv; educational expenses of, 88–90, 97, 98, 104; economic independence of, xi, xvii, 12, 68–72, 78, 81; employment of, xvi–xvii, 15–16, 67–69, 70, 72–73, 77–81, 95, 100, 104, 112–113; family support for, 95, 101–102, 112; housing conditions of, 61–67, 84–85, 95; household budgets of, 62, 63–64, 85–90, 96, 98, 99–100; income of, xvii, 15–16, 68, 73, 74–77, 78, 87; motherhood and, 13, 14, 16, 83, 93, 99, 102–105, 113–115; social class and, xi–xii, xiii, xv, xix, 16, 66, 85, 93, 96–97, 101–105, 107, 111–112, 113–115; social movements of, xv; university graduates among, 69–72, 90, 94–99, 104; work-family balance of, xii, 67–68, 69, 69–70, 71–72, 73–74, 80–81, 83, 90–92, 98, 100–101, 103, 112; work participation rate of, xvi, 94. *See also* Bubble generation; pre-Bubble generation
social class, xvii; gender and, xii, xvii–xix, xx–xxi, 34, 77, 107–111, 113–115. *See also* cultural capital; family ideal; motherhood; single mothers

social policy, gender and, 6–7, 16; single mothers and, xiv–xvi, 12–14
stay-at-home mothers. *See* housewife

unmarried single mothers, xiv, xxi, 56–59, 62

widowed mothers, xiv, xv, xxi
widowed mothers' pension (*boshi nenkin*), xvi

Vogel, Ezra, 1, 2

White, Merry, 37

Yamada, Masahiro, xi
Yokoyama, Fumino, 6
Yoshizumi, Kyoko, 52, 53

About the Author

Aya Ezawa is a university lecturer in the Sociology of Japan at Leiden University in the Netherlands.